How to CREATE AND SAVE A FORTUNE Using Life Insurance

Life Insurance... The 1% Solution

Why not let 1% of your estate or business protect the other 99%?

HOWARD WIGHT

Dedication

To my children, David and Jennifer, whom I love very much, and who have paid a very high price for whatever success I may have achieved. And to Ben Feldman, John Savage, Frank Sullivan, Tom Wolff, and Jim Herrington whose ideas have made a difference in my life.

Acknowledgments

In addition to all the people whose ideas have formed the basis of this book, I would like to especially thank Debra Ackerman for her hard work, patience, and persistence, and Gary Craig for his input and insights.

ISBN 0-9633506-3-3

Lexington House

Publishers of America's Finest Books

98 Dennis Drive
Lexington, KY 40503

Table of Contents

NO! I CAN'T BE BOTHERED TO SEE ANY PESKY SALESMAN....I'VE GOT A BATTLE TO FIGHT!

Introduction

My goal in writing this book is to make life insurance easy to understand . . . to make it user-friendly. Most people are uncomfortable when it comes to the subject of death. As a result, many of them do what they can to avoid its discussion.

You are going to die. No one has a lease on life. If you don't die before age 65 . . . you are going to die after age 65. This is not said to frighten you. It is stated in order for us to come to grips with reality. You are not immortal. You would not be reading a book about life insurance if you were.

Many people tend to treat life insurance as an expense to be minimized. I view life insurance as an asset to be optimized within the context of your overall financial situation. You either have an estate size problem or an estate tax problem. An estate size problem means that you have not had the time to create an estate large enough to provide for yourself and your family. An estate tax problem means that you have an estate large enough to provide for your family, but the estate is, therefore, large enough to be subject to estate taxes.

Life insurance can create a fortune for your family. It can help create a fortune to supplement your own retirement income. When you have created a fortune, life insurance can save that fortune from being devastated by estate taxes and related costs.

Now, let me show you ***how to create and save a fortune using life insurance***.

Howard Wight
December, 1996

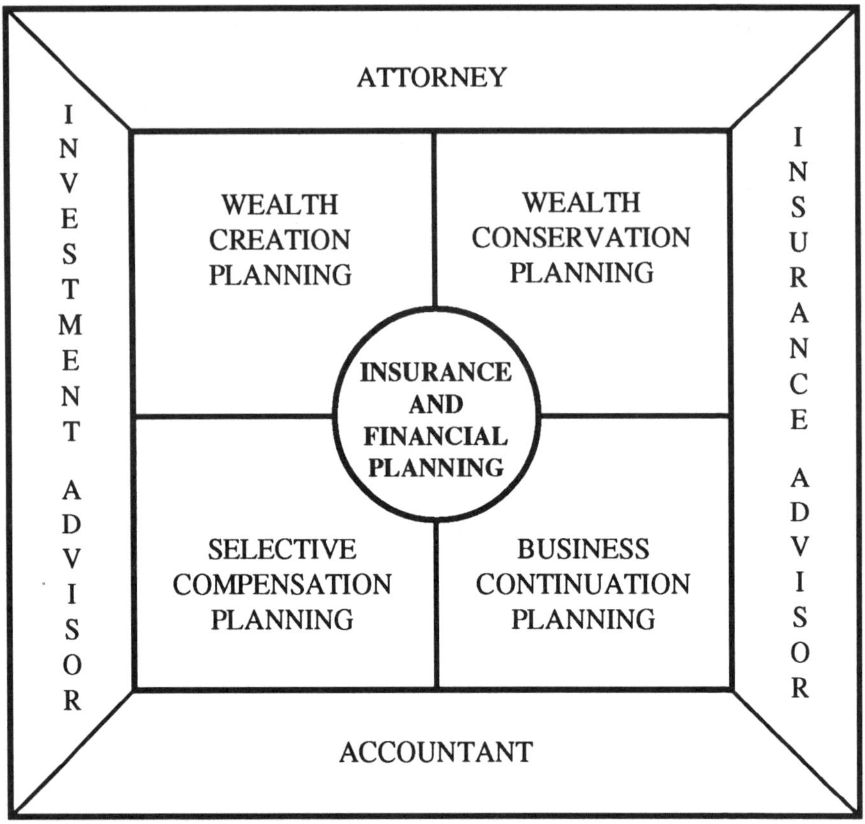

This diagram is intended to give you an overview of the areas included in insurance and financial planning. Because life insurance is essential in each of these areas, it is frequently the insurance agent who will be the catalyst and coordinator in developing and implementing a comprehensive strategy.

☞ CHAPTER 1 ☜

❑

Overview

The purpose of this book is to enable you to make smart, informed decisions regarding your life insurance program. I want to help you help your life insurance agent do the best possible job for you and your family.

Most people do piecemeal planning when it comes to financial planning. They typically spend more time planning their annual vacation than they do planning their financial future. Overall insurance and financial planning basically boils down to the four areas shown in the diagram on Page 2:

- ❑ Wealth Creation Planning (Chapter 2)
- ❑ Wealth Conservation Planning (Chapter 3)
- ❑ Business Continuation Planning (Chapter 4)
- ❑ Selective Compensation Planning (Chapter 5)

In order to develop a coordinated and comprehensive investment and insurance strategy (see the diagram on Page 4), it is important to realize that life insurance is the cornerstone in building a firm foundation for your family's financial future.

Investment and Insurance Strategy

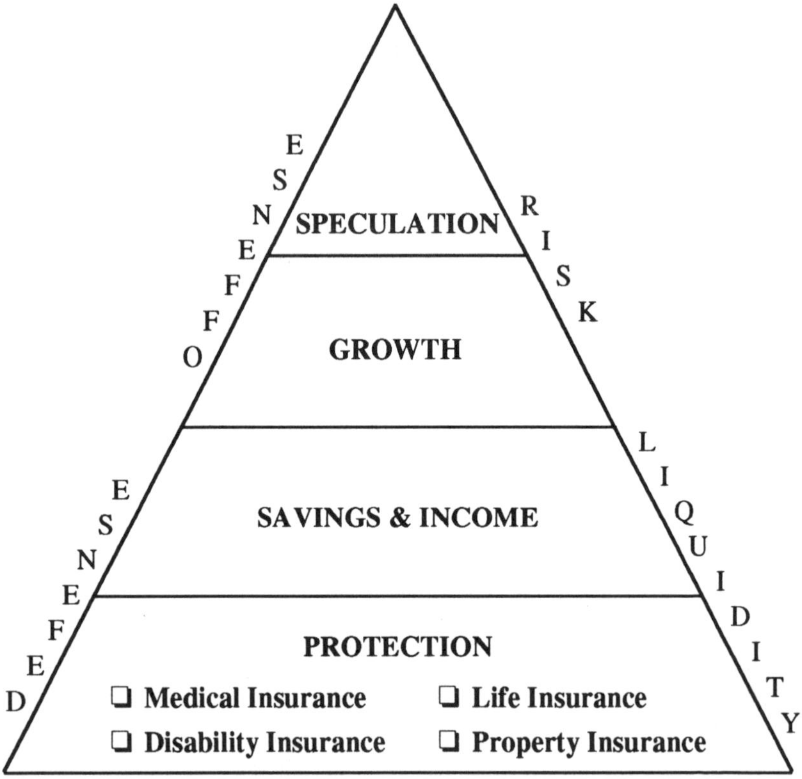

In professional football, a team does not go to the Super Bowl unless it has both a great offense and a great defense. You cannot develop a sound financial strategy for your family without having a sound defense. Life insurance is the greatest defensive tool available in the financial marketplace.

❑ THE ROLE OF YOUR LIFE INSURANCE AGENT

Because life insurance plays such a major role in each of the areas mentioned above, the life insurance agent is the logical choice to be the catalyst and coordinator in developing and implementing an overall plan. It does you and your family no good to develop the world's greatest plan unless you implement it. One of the roles your agent plays is that of financial conscience. He or she has the tough role of getting you to discuss death and other topics you may be reluctant to talk about, and then urging you to take the necessary action. Because circumstances change, your agent should also be responsible for reviewing your situation with you annually, or at least every two years.

❑ THE PLANNING PROCESS

The planning process consists of the following phases:

Phase I	The Situation (Assessing Where You Are Now)
Phase II	Determining Your Goals and Priorities
Phase III	Pinpointing Problems and Opportunities
Phase IV	Presenting Options
Phase V	Selecting the Solutions
Phase VI	Taking Action and Implementing the Solutions
Phase VII	Achieving Results
Phase VIII	Reviewing the Results

Planning is an ongoing process . . . not a one-time event. Once you finish . . . you review, refine, and revise. Completing the *Financial Statement* on Page 6 and answering

Financial Statement as of ______________

ASSETS:	
RESIDENCE	
CASH ACCOUNTS	
CASH VALUE	
STOCKS AND BONDS	
REAL ESTATE INVESTMENTS	
OTHER INVESTMENTS	
BUSINESS	
RETIREMENT PLANS	
OTHER ASSETS	
TOTAL ASSETS	
LIABILITIES:	
RESIDENCE MORTGAGE	
OTHER MORTGAGES	
CASH VALUE LOANS	
MARGIN ACCOUNT	
OTHER LIABILITIES	
TOTAL LIABILITIES	
NET WORTH	

the questions that appear on Pages 8 and 9 will give you a head start in helping you and your agent to develop a plan.

❑ PRIMARY FINANCIAL CONCERNS

Most people are primarily concerned about the following:

- ❑ Death – Will their family have enough money if they die prematurely?
- ❑ Disability – Will they and their family have enough money if they are disabled?
- ❑ Retirement – Will they have adequate money to enable them to lead a comfortable retirement without fear of running out of money?
- ❑ Estate Planning – How can they ensure that their money gets to their intended heirs and how can they minimize the impact of estate taxes and related costs?

If they own a business, many of them are additionally concerned about:

- ❑ Business Continuation Planning – Who will own and run the business and what impact will their death have on the business?
- ❑ Selective Compensation Planning – How do you recruit, retain, and reward key people?

FINANCIAL FOCUS

- ❑ What role does money play in your life? What's important about money to you?
- ❑ What are your plans regarding retirement? What are you doing to accomplish your plans?
- ❑ What types of investments do you favor? Why?
- ❑ What are your investment results over the past five years? Are you pleased?
- ❑ Would you be pleased with the same results over the next five years? What would you do differently?
- ❑ How much time do you spend selecting and managing your investments? How much is your time worth?
- ❑ Do you feel you can outperform someone who spends all of his or her time managing investments?
- ❑ What would happen to you and your family if your income were to stop today?
- ❑ What have you done to enable your family to have an adequate income in the event of your death?
- ❑ Have you provided a cash cushion for emergencies, education funding, etc.?
- ❑ What role does life insurance play in your financial plans, both personally and in your business?
- ❑ How much life insurance do you have? How did you decide on the amount? The type? The company? The agent?
- ❑ To what extent are your spouse and children involved in your financial decision making?
- ❑ What advisors do you use and to what extent?
- ❑ How did you get started in your business?
- ❑ What makes your business different from the competition? What problems do you foresee?
- ❑ What are your plans for your business at your retirement or death or disability?

FINANCIAL FOCUS

- ❑ What steps have you taken to accomplish your plans for your business?
- ❑ To what extent are your children involved in your business?
- ❑ Who will ultimately run your business? What are you doing to retain and reward them?
- ❑ What are you doing in terms of selective compensation plans for yourself and your key people?
- ❑ What impact would the loss of key people have on sales, profits, lines of credit, retirement plans, and stock value?
- ❑ How much vacation do you take? What impact would it have on your business if you were gone for six months? Or forever?
- ❑ Where do you want your money to go when you die?
- ❑ How do you feel about your children receiving a large inheritance? Why?
- ❑ When did you last update your will(s) and trust(s)?
- ❑ What is the approximate value of your estate?
- ❑ What is the potential estate tax impact and what have you done about it? How will the estate taxes be paid?
- ❑ To what extent have you made gifts to your children or considered doing so?
- ❑ What are your thoughts regarding giving or leaving assets to a favorite charity or to your community?
- ❑ If you knew you only had six months to live, what changes would you make? What if you had died last week?
- ❑ How do you want to be remembered by your children? Grandchildren? Employees? Community?
- ❑ What are your primary concerns and goals and why? What's really important to you?
- ❑ What would you like to accomplish as a result of our discussions? Who else should be involved?

❑ THE ROLE OF LIFE INSURANCE

Life insurance will help you accomplish the following:

- ❑ It will help provide an adequate income for your family if you die prematurely.
- ❑ It will provide a cash cushion for emergencies.
- ❑ It will provide cash to help educate your children.
- ❑ It will provide cash to pay estate taxes when you have a large estate.
- ❑ It will provide supplemental retirement benefits.

Most of us were told when we were growing up that we should put away money for a rainy day. Almost everyone encounters times when they wish they had more cash in order to handle emergencies or unforeseen needs or to take advantage of investment opportunities. Life insurance is a super-simple systematic savings plan which will help you cope with the financial contingencies we all encounter in life.

❑ WHY BUY LIFE INSURANCE?

People buy life insurance because they care about someone or something (for example, a favorite charity), or because they owe someone.

If you don't have an estate tax problem, you probably have an estate size problem. In either case, life insurance can help. This book will help you explore the many ways life insurance can help you not only **create a fortune**, but also how it can help you **save a fortune** from estate taxes and related costs.

No one has a lease on life. If you don't die before age 65, you will die after age 65. When you die, there will be an emotional loss felt by those you leave behind, but beyond the emotional loss is the economic loss which will be suffered. If your death will create an economic loss for your family, your business, your estate, your community, your church or temple, your college, your school, or your favorite charity, you probably need some more life insurance.

The diagram on Page 12 will give you an overview of why people buy life insurance and the subjects that we will be addressing in the remainder of this book.

- ❑ **WHAT MOST PEOPLE WANT TO KNOW ABOUT LIFE INSURANCE**
  - ❑ Why should I buy life insurance?
  - ❑ How much life insurance do I need?
  - ❑ What type should I buy?
  - ❑ How much will it cost?
  - ❑ From whom should I buy it?
  - ❑ When should I buy it?

Let's now explore the answers to these questions.

Life Insurance Overview
Personal Planning
Income Continuation
Pay Off Liabilities
Education Fund
Emergency Cash Cushion
Special Bequests
Charitable Bequests
Estate Tax Funding
Business Planning
Buy & Sell Funding
Key Management Loss
Pay Off Loans
Salary Continuation
Selective Compensation Plans
Insurance Options
Do Nothing
Term Insurance
Cash Value Insurance
Combination

☞ CHAPTER 2 ☜

❑

How to Create a Fortune Using Life Insurance

WEALTH CREATION PLANNING

❑ THE MONEY MACHINE

If you owned a money machine that printed $200,000 per year of legal, spendable U.S. dollars, would you insure the money machine? Of course you would! If you owned the goose that laid the golden eggs, would you insure the goose? Of course you would! For how much?

You are the money machine. You are the goose that lays the golden eggs.

❑ HOW TO CREATE A FORTUNE FOR YOUR FAMILY

What your family needs is a backup money machine. That's where life insurance comes in. Let's take a look

How Life Insurance Works

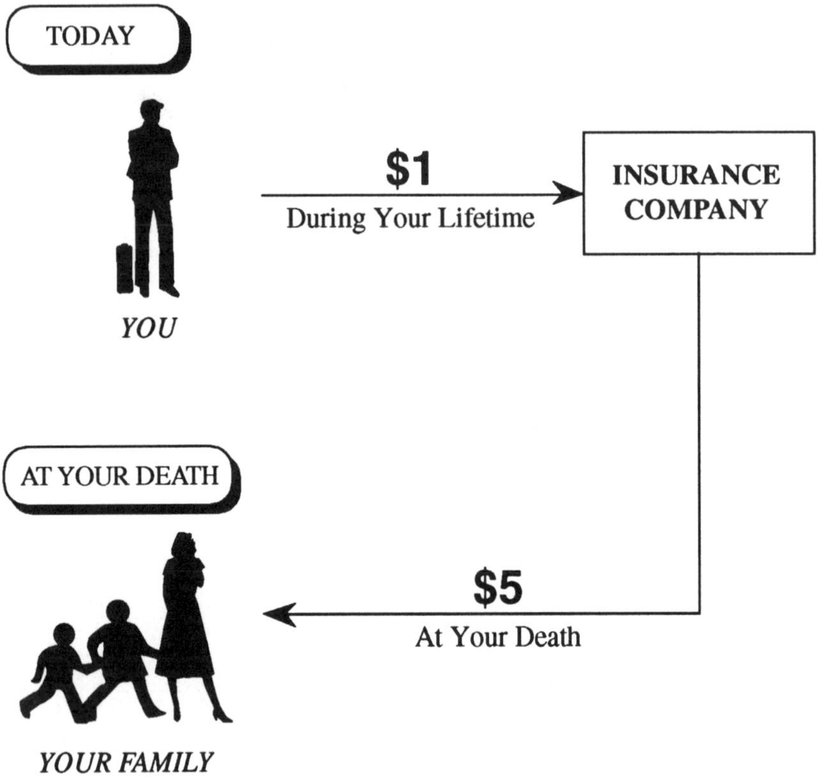

Note: The actual premium and death benefit amounts are determined by the specifics of the individual's age and health and the plan of insurance selected.

at the diagram on Page 14. You pay the premium to the insurance company. When you die, the insurance company pays the income tax-free death benefit to your family. To facilitate an understanding of the concept, let's use some numbers. You pay $1 to the insurance company, and when you die, the insurance company pays $5 to your family. That is the essence of how life insurance works. You pay $100,000 to the insurance company, and when you die, the insurance company pays $500,000 to your family.

But let's assume you don't want to pay $100,000 right now to the insurance company. The insurance company will finance the premium for you. You can pay anywhere from a few hundred dollars per year up to a few thousand dollars per year. The amount you pay is based on your age and health and whether you want term insurance or cash value insurance, or a combination. What type of insurance and how much it costs is discussed in more detail in Chapter 7.

❑ HOW MUCH IS A FORTUNE?

You decide. How much do you want your family to have in the event of your death? How much will they need? If you own a business, how much money will it need?

Life Insurance Summary for Robert Sample

ANNUAL PREMIUM: $10,000 (AGE 35)

END OF YEAR	AGE	TOTAL PREMIUMS	CASH VALUE	DEATH BENEFIT
1	36	$10,000	$5,823	$1,000,000
5	40	50,000	44,767	1,000,000
10	45	100,000	117,489	1,000,000
20	55	200,000	382,325	1,000,000
30	65	300,000	947,499	1,571,495

SUMMARY ASSUMING DEATH AT AGE 85

Annual Retirement Benefit (Age 65-85) $57,400

Total Retirement Income (Age 65-85) 1,148,000

Tax-Free Death Benefit (Age 85) 1,382,928

Total Benefits $2,530,928

Total Cost $300,000

These figures are based on current assumptions and are not guaranteed.

This plan is self-completing if you are disabled.

Flexible Funding Options

- ❑ Do It Yourself
- ❑ Corporate Funding
- ❑ Combination

❑ HOW TO CREATE A FORTUNE FOR YOURSELF AND YOUR FAMILY

Until now, we have been discussing creating a fortune just for your family in the event of your death. Let's now take a look at cash value life insurance.

> *Cash Value Puts the Life Into Life Insurance.*

Let's look at the summary on Page 16. Now let's highlight the key points:

Annual Retirement Benefit (starting at age 65) $57,400
Pre-Retirement Death Benefit $1,000,000
The Plan is Self-Completing if You are Disabled

Summary Assuming Death at Age 85

Total Retirement Income (Age 65-85) $1,148,000
Death Benefit Paid to Your Family (Age 85) 1,382,928
Total Benefits $2,530,928

Annual Premium.. $10,000
Total Premiums $300,000

With this plan, you will have created a fortune both for yourself and your family! How does this sound to you? What do you think? If you were now age 65 and looking back, wouldn't you be glad you had the foresight to start this plan at age 35?

Why Not Beat The Bank?

$10,000 ANNUAL DEPOSIT/PREMIUM STARTING AT AGE 35	THE BANK*	LIFE INSURANCE
INITIAL DEATH BENEFIT	**$10,000**	**$1,000,000**
10-YEAR SUMMARY (AGE 45)		
Deposits/Premiums	$100,000	$100,000
Cash – Alive	126,270	117,489
Cash – Dead	126,270	1,000,000
20-YEAR SUMMARY (AGE 55)		
Deposits/Premiums	$200,000	$200,000
Cash – Alive	316,806	382,325
Cash – Dead	316,806	1,000,000
30-YEAR SUMMARY (AGE 65)		
Deposits/Premiums	$300,000	$300,000
Cash – Alive	604,318	947,499
Cash – Dead	604,318	1,571,495

These figures are based on current assumptions and are not guaranteed.

* Assumes Certificates of Deposit Paying 7% Interest, 40% Marginal Tax Bracket (Federal and State), 4.2% Net.

Which Scenario Do You Prefer?

A key point to understand is that the cash value of an insurance policy accumulates on a tax-deferred basis and can be withdrawn from the policy by borrowing so that there is no income tax on the withdrawals. Or the dividends can be used to provide a retirement income, in which case, the income is taxable.

❑ WHY NOT BEAT THE BANK?

The only way you can really start to understand how good something is . . . is to compare it to something else. Let's now look at the chart on Page 18. Most people have no idea how great cash value insurance is in terms of accumulating money.

> *I am convinced that almost everyone, if they truly understood life insurance, would be lining up to buy it.*

❑ "BUT I HAVE ALWAYS HEARD THAT LIFE INSURANCE IS A LOUSY INVESTMENT"

You be the judge. We compare term insurance with cash value insurance in Chapter 7. We compare buying term and investing the difference. We also mention variable life insurance, which is a type of life insurance policy which enables you to invest in what are essentially mutual funds. You can basically design your insurance policy to take whatever degree of risk you are willing to assume. The key point to remember is that you are buying life insurance primarily for security, protection, and peace of mind . . . not for excitement.

"I am now, and I always have been, a believer in life insurance . . . even a poor man can build up an estate with life insurance. When he does create such an estate, he can feel real satisfaction in knowing that his family is protected if anything happens."

HARRY S. TRUMAN

☞ CHAPTER 3 ☜

How to Save a Fortune Using Life Insurance

WEALTH CONSERVATION AND ESTATE PLANNING

How do you create a small fortune? Subject a large fortune to estate taxes. When will your stock portfolio drop 50% in value? The day you die, it will effectively drop 50% in value because of the estate taxes which will be due within nine months in cash.

Your estate is the tangible representation of your lifetime. Estate taxes are a ticking time bomb which will devastate your estate unless you have life insurance to pay the estate taxes. You can invest 30, 40, or 50 years building an estate, and without proper prior planning,

Where Do You Want Your Money To Go?

Rank in order of preference where you want your money to go:

________ IRS ESTATE TAX COLLECTOR

________ YOUR CHILDREN

________ YOUR GRANDCHILDREN

________ YOUR FAVORITE CHARITY

the IRS Estate Tax Collector can tear it apart virtually overnight.

You may be aware that you can leave your entire estate to your spouse without triggering estate taxes. I am addressing this chapter to those people who want their estate to go to their children, their grandchildren, or their favorite charity, rather than to the IRS.

Most people want to know what time it is . . . not how to build a clock. With that in mind, I am going to avoid getting involved in explaining the intricacies of trusts and estate planning. Your insurance agent can help coordinate your estate and insurance planning with an attorney who specializes in estate planning. It should be readily apparent that as you read this book, if you need life insurance and estate planning, your attorney is probably not a specialist in these areas or he would have already brought the need for planning to your attention.

Let's take a look at the *The Tax on Success* chart on Page 24. A married couple worth $5,000,000 would have a potential estate tax liability of $1,868,000. By the time you add the related expenses which would include attorneys' fees, accountants' fees, appraisal fees, state inheritance taxes (if any), funeral expenses, medical expenses, etc., you could be looking at total taxes and expenses of about $2,000,000, or about 40% of the $5,000,000.

THE TAX ON SUCCESS
ESTATE TAX CHART

	SINGLE TAXPAYER		MARRIED COUPLE	
			TAX PAID AT SECOND DEATH	
ESTATE VALUE	ESTATE TAX	% OF ESTATE	ESTATE TAX	% OF ESTATE
$1,000,000	$153,000	15%	$ 0	0%
1,200,000	235,000	20%	0	0%
1,500,000	363,000	24%	114,000	8%
2,000,000	588,000	29%	320,000	16%
2,500,000	833,000	33%	543,000	22%
3,000,000	1,098,000	37%	784,000	26%
4,000,000	1,648,000	41%	1,318,000	33%
5,000,000	2,198,000	44%	1,868,000	37%
7,500,000	3,573,000	48%	3,243,000	43%
10,000,000	4,948,000	49%	4,618,000	46%
15,000,000	7,948,000	53%	7,588,000	51%
20,000,000	10,948,000	55%	10,588,000	53%
30,000,000	16,500,000	55%	16,170,000	54%
50,000,000	27,500,000	55%	27,170,000	54%
100,000,000	55,000,000	55%	54,670,000	55%

The estate must be valued as of the date of death or six months later. Taxes are due and payable in cash within nine months after the date of death. This could result in the costly liquidation of valuable growth and income-producing assets unless adequate cash is available. Many wealthy people prefer to use life insurance to pay the estate taxes at a substantial discount.

For a married couple, $600,000 is placed in a unified credit trust or is left outright to the children at the first death. The $600,000 therefore escapes taxation at both deaths, as does any growth on the $600,000. The balance of the estate is taxed at the second death.

A number of experts in the field of estate planning have referred to the deferral of estate taxes until the second death as a "sucker play." The deferral gives people a false sense of security. Failure to plan will still result in the unnecessary liquidation of assets. The deferral will also result in more taxes having to be paid if the assets grow. It, therefore, sometimes makes sense to pay the estate tax at the first death.

Could You Write a Check Today for up to 50% or More of Everything You Own?

If your estate continues to grow, the tax will continue to grow. By the time your estate is worth $10,000,000, the estate taxes and related costs will approximate $5,000,000, or 50% of the $10,000,000.

Could you write a check today for 50% or more of everything you own without it hurting just a little bit? Of course not! If you can't write that check, how are your children going to write that check?

> *Why not let 1% of your estate help protect the other 99%?*

If your estate is now worth $10,000,000, let's take 1%, or $100,000, and purchase $5,000,000 of insurance. Doesn't it make more sense to set aside 1% per year rather than be faced with the forced liquidation of 50% all at once? Wouldn't you rather use the insurance company's money to pay what has to be paid rather than using your money? Wouldn't you prefer to have your estate go to your children rather than to 260,000,000 strangers? Let's face facts. The IRS is not going to put up a building with your name on it, so let's not give the IRS any more of your money than you absolutely have to. Doesn't that make sense?

As I stated earlier, if your estate keeps growing, the estate tax will keep growing. A major question that you

"Buy enough life insurance to cover your estate taxes.

However stiff the premium might seem, it's a bargain."

FORTUNE, March 18, 1996
"How to Leave the Tax Man Nothing"
by Eileen P. Gunn

need to address is whether you should buy enough insurance to handle the tax problem only for today, or into the foreseeable future.

❑ WHAT ARE YOUR OPTIONS WHEN IT COMES TO PAYING ESTATE TAXES?

You essentially have five options with regard to the source of money for paying estate taxes:

- ❑ Sell or Liquidate Your Assets
- ❑ Set Aside a Large Cash Reserve
- ❑ Borrow the Money
- ❑ Buy Life Insurance
- ❑ Use A Combination of the Above

You will note that each of the first three methods ultimately results in losing the asset plus interest. For example, if stocks had to be sold, the stocks would be lost, but so would any future growth and income. Using a large cash reserve would result in the loss of the cash and the interest it would have earned in the future. Borrowing the money, which may not even be possible or practical, would result in repaying the principal plus interest. Every other method of paying estate taxes results in the loss of principal plus interest. With life insurance, you pay interest only . . . in advance.

Most everyone hates taxes and dislikes insurance. Why not use something you dislike to pay something you hate? In that context, life insurance is the lesser of two evils.

Occasionally, I will encounter a situation where an attorney or accountant accepts the need for life insurance when the estate is basically illiquid, such as when the estate consists primarily of real estate or a closely-held business. However, if the estate is mostly liquid, being primarily invested in stocks, bonds, or certificates of deposit, etc., these same advisors feel there is no need for insurance. Does that make any sense to you? It makes no sense to me whatsoever. If someone is worth $10,000,000, they either want their estate to go to their children, or they don't. It has little to do with the question of liquidity.

> *Estate taxes are a ticking time bomb that will devastate your estate.*

❑ THE OWNERSHIP OF INSURANCE FOR ESTATE TAX PURPOSES

Most people are familiar with the fact that an insurance policy has an owner and a beneficiary (or beneficiaries). Most are not familiar with the fact that there is also an owner of the policy. Quite often, the insured is the owner. In estate planning, where the purpose of the insurance is to pay the estate taxes, having the insured as the owner would be disastrous from a tax standpoint.

Again, let's say for example, that you are worth $10,000,000, and that you have decided to purchase $5,000,000 of insurance to pay the estate taxes. Everything that you own will be included in your estate. That means that from a tax standpoint, if you own the insurance, your estate is now worth $15,000,000 rather than $10,000,000. Estate taxes and related costs would then be about $7,500,000 rather than $5,000,000. The solution to this problem is to make your children or an irrevocable trust the owner of the policy. This is why it is so important to have a good insurance agent. He or she will coordinate this with your attorney.

❑ SECOND-TO-DIE INSURANCE POLICIES

Because a married couple can elect to defer the estate taxes until both spouses have died, some smart marketing people at the insurance companies developed special policies which insured both spouses, but which did not pay until both had died. This meant that the policies could have a dramatically lower premium because two people had to die rather than one.

This may be the best type of policy in your situation and it may not. If you have assets which are expected to grow rapidly in terms of value, it may be best to elect to pay taxes at the first death while the asset value is lower, rather than deferring the tax until the second death when the tax might be significantly higher. Again, your agent can help you decide what is best in your specific situation. One size does not fit all. The best solution must be tailored to the specifics of the situation.

❑ UNMARRIED COUPLES

If you are not married, you can't defer the estate taxes until the second death. Therefore, it makes preeminently good sense to acquire life insurance to help offset the impact of estate taxes.

❑ HOW TO KEEP MORE BY GIVING IT AWAY

Are you aware that an individual can make gifts of $10,000 annually to anyone they choose? For example, a married couple having two children could give a total of $40,000 annually. If they had two grandchildren, they could give another $40,000 annually. The amounts given each year would no longer be included in the estate of the parents, nor would the future growth on the gifts be included.

Additionally, during your lifetime, you can give away another $600,000 without there being any gift tax. A married couple, in addition to the gifts mentioned above, could give their children an additional $1,200,000 and pay no gift taxes.

These types of planning decisions are the kind that a lot of people would welcome.

Gifts are often the sources of the premiums to pay for insurance to pay the estate taxes.

Let's look at a situation where life insurance can both create and save a fortune (see chart on Page 32). Let's revisit our married couple who are worth $10,000,000. They would like their children and grandchildren to receive as much of their estate as possible. They also can conceive of no circumstances when they would miss the "top $1,000,000." From their perspective, the "top $1,000,000" is "extra money." They are willing to gift it in order to purchase insurance for the benefit of their children and/or grandchildren.

If they were to keep the "top $1,000,000," about 50%, or $500,000 of that $1,000,000, would go to estate taxes. Gifting the $1,000,000 and using it to purchase life insurance might enable them to purchase $10,000,000 of insurance with that single payment. Because the $10,000,000 is not subject to estate taxes, the children or grandchildren would receive the entire $10,000,000.

Instead of making the gift and purchasing $10,000,000 of insurance, let's assume our couple retains the $1,000,000 and invests it. $1,000,000 would have to grow to $20,000,000 in order for the children and grandchildren to net $10,000,000. How long would it take for $1,000,000 to grow to $20,000,000? At 7% compounded net-after-taxes, it would take 45 years.

The Top Million

When you have a multi-million-dollar estate, the top $1,000,000 may not make a meaningful difference in your life. Its presence or absence is not going to affect your standard of living one iota. It might even be called "extra money," if there could be such a thing. When you die, about 60% of the $1,000,000 and any growth on the $1,000,000 will go to estate taxes and related costs.

Let's examine two alternative strategies.

PLAN A: The top million is retained in your estate and grows. At 7% compounded, the $1,000,000 will grow to $5,000,000 in 24 years, but if you were to die at that point in time, about $3,000,000 would go to estate taxes and related costs, and your children would receive only about $2,000,000.

Likewise, if you were to live 35 years, the top million will have grown to $10,000,000, but of that, only about $4,000,000 will get to your children.

Retaining the top million in your estate and investing it would not seem to be especially effective.

Let's explore another option.

PLAN B: The top million could be gifted to your children or to an irrevocable trust, so that all the growth would be outside of your estate and thus not subject to estate taxes at your death. The top million could then be used to purchase life insurance. The specific amount purchased would be contingent on the plan selected, age, and health.

In the example, the top million is shown being used to purchase $10,000,000 of insurance. If it were used to purchase only $5,000,000, the bottom-line results are still better than Plan A.

Which Plan Do You Prefer?

PLAN A
$10,000,000

$6,000,000
Estate Taxes
and
Related Costs

$4,000,000
to
Your Children

$1,000,000

PLAN B
$10,000,000

$10,000,000
to
Your Children

$1,000,000

> *The leverage of life insurance is incredible, wouldn't you agree?*

If the $1,000,000 could only purchase $5,000,000 rather than $10,000,000 of insurance, the results are still astonishing. $1,000,000, if invested, would have to grow to $10,000,000 in order for the children and grandchildren to net $5,000,000. At 7%, it would take 35 years.

❑ WHAT IF CONGRESS DOES AWAY WITH THE ESTATE TAX?

What if you have purchased life insurance to pay estate taxes, and the law is changed to do away with the estate tax? Your children will receive more money, or the "extra money" can be given to your favorite charity, or you (and your spouse) can attempt to spend more during your lifetime in order to offset the unanticipated surplus. Does this really sound like a problem? Buy life insurance based on the current law . . . not based on trying to guess what might happen in the future.

❑ CONCLUSION

You cannot have an estate tax problem without having the premium which is the solution to the problem. Let's put the premium and the problem in perspective. Compared to the problem, the premium is almost always peanuts. Why not let 1% (or 2%) each year protect the other 99% (or 98%)? If your estate is growing at the rate of say 5% per year, we are merely slowing the growth a little. When your estate is large enough to be subject to estate taxes, it is important to understand that 50% or more of the future growth is earmarked for estate taxes. Why not let part of the growth which would be lost to estate taxes anyhow be used to protect your estate?

> *Why not let life insurance create a fence around your fortune?*

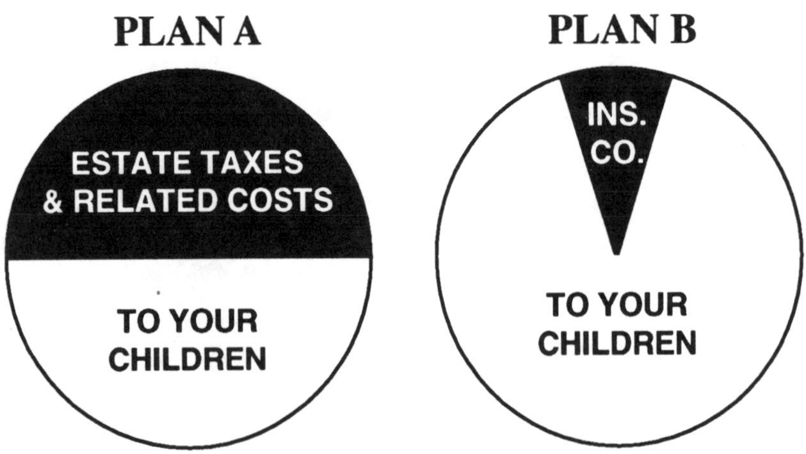

Which Plan Do You Prefer?

☞ CHAPTER 4 ☜

❑ *Business Continuation Planning*

The death of a business owner presents the following potential problems:

- ❑ Income Continuation. How will the deceased owner's family be able to draw funds from the business in order to replace his salary? Can the business afford to make payments to the decedent's family without his being there to contribute to the ongoing profitability of the business?
- ❑ Buy and Sell Funding. Should the deceased owner's family continue to own an interest in a business in which they are not involved? Would the surviving owner(s) want to be in business with the decedent's family and its advisors?
- ❑ Key Management Loss. What will be the impact of the owner's death on the survivors' personal and

Business Needs Analysis

POTENTIAL CAPITAL REQUIREMENTS	NOW	FUTURE
❑ **FUNDING A BUY AND SELL AGREEMENT** to purchase the decedent's interest in the business without creating a cash drain on the business and uncertainty for the decedent's family.	$500,000	$1,000,000
❑ **OFFSETTING THE KEY MANAGEMENT LOSS** impact on working capital, sales, profits, growth, credit lines, retirement plans, etc., without creating a cash drain and unnecessary uncertainty for the business and survivors.	$1,000,000	$1,000,000
❑ **PROVIDING SALARY CONTINUATION** to the decedent's family (example, fifty percent of salary per year for ten years).	$1,000,000	$1,500,000
❑ **PAYING ESTATE TAXES AT A DISCOUNT** and avoiding the costly and unnecessary liquidation of valuable growth and income-producing assets.	–	?
TOTAL POTENTIAL CAPITAL REQUIREMENTS	$2,500,000	$3,500,000
CAPITAL NOW AVAILABLE	–	–
POTENTIAL CAPITAL SHORTAGE	**$2,500,000**	**$3,500,000**

Why not acquire business-funded life insurance to provide cash at the exact moment it is most needed? Why not let the business help solve the problems it helps create? Why not let the event which creates the problems be the event which creates the solution?

business plans and on the business' sales, profits, growth, working capital, credit lines, and retirement plans, etc.?

- ❑ Estate Tax Funding. How will the deceased owner's children pay the estate taxes without being forced to liquidate valuable growth and income-producing assets? How will the decedent's estate be divided fairly among his children?

> *Why not let death, the event*
> *which creates the problems,*
> *be the event which creates the solution?*

❑ BUSINESS NEEDS ANALYSIS AND KEY EXECUTIVE VALUATION

The *Business Needs Analysis* on Page 36 and the *Key Executive Valuation* worksheet on Page 38 will help you and your agent determine how much insurance you need in connection with these areas.

❑ FAMILY BUSINESS CONTINUATION PLANNING

When you want to keep a family-owned business in the family, there are a number of factors which should be considered. The primary issues can be broken down into

Key Executive Valuation

		Example	
Key Executive's Current Salary		$100,000	
Total Salary Compensation for Management Group		200,000	
Executive's Salary as % of Total Management Compensation		50%	
REPLACEMENT COST (TRANSITION AND TRAINING)			
Replacement Executive's Salary*		$150,000	
Current Executive's Salary		100,000	
Additional Outlay		50,000	
Transition Period (Years)		x 3	
Total Additional Salary		150,000	
Fee to Executive Recruiter ($150,000 x 20%)		30,000	
Replacement Cost	(A)	$180,000	
POTENTIAL IMPACT ON SALES			
Anticipated Sales for 3 Years		$3,000,000	
% Attributed to Current Executive		50%	
Sales Attributed to Current Key Executive		1,500,000	
Assumed 50% Reduction	(B)	$750,000	
POTENTIAL IMPACT ON CREDIT LINES			
Anticipated Line of Credit		$1,000,000	
Attributed to Current Executive		50%	
Potential Credit Line Loss	(C)	500,000	
TOTAL KEY EXECUTIVE VALUATION (A+B+C)		$1,430,000	

*The replacement executive's compensation may have to be substantially higher if he does not have an equity ownership position.

two basic categories . . . the people problems and the money problems.

People Problems

- ❑ Which family members will be involved in the business?
- ❑ Which family members will control the business?
- ❑ Which family members will manage the business?
- ❑ How do the family members get along?
- ❑ How will the estate be divided fairly (not necessarily equally) among the children?
- ❑ Should the children's spouses and children ultimately own stock?

Money Problems

- ❑ What impact will the death of a family member have on the business?
- ❑ What impact will estate taxes have on the business and the rest of the estate?
- ❑ Will the business have adequate operating capital?
- ❑ Will the business be able to pay off existing loans?
- ❑ Will the business have adequate lines of credit?
- ❑ Will the business be able to pay income to family members?
- ❑ Will the business be able to buy out family members who want out?
- ❑ Will the business be able to recruit, reward, and retain key managers?

While some families consider these issues before they become problems, in many cases, death is the event which triggers the problems. If not planned for, these issues can easily escalate into major problems which will diminish the probability of the business being able to continue in a favorable environment. If not provided for, the money issues can make the interpersonal issues even tougher to deal with.

While every situation is unique, experience would lead us to certain common-sense conclusions. Those not actively involved in the business should probably not own stock in the business. They will want to get as much money as possible out of the business. Those family members actively involved in the business will want to keep as much money in the business as possible. One child should probably be designated to run the business, as committees don't generally work.

The estate tax can have a major negative impact on everything. The estate taxes and related costs will approximate 50% or more of the total estate value. Most estates don't contain this type of liquidity. Even if they did, it would still make more sense to use life insurance, which would typically result in discounting the cost of paying the estate tax by 80% or more.

Life insurance can also provide the cash to be used to pay off loans, offset the loss of sales, buy out family members, equalize the estate among the children, and provide selective benefits for key managers. The death of a business owner creates certain problems which can best be solved with cash. Life insurance is cash . . . exactly when needed. Why not let death, the event which creates the problems, be the event which creates the solution?

Most people don't like to think about dying, much less think about life insurance. The failure to think about both will normally result in an additional death . . . the death of the business.

Life insurance is a common-sense cash cushion. It is a super-simple, systematic, supplemental savings and accumulation plan for retirement, education, emergencies, and investment opportunities . . . coupled with protection for your family and business.

Key Executive Bonus Plan Overview
(Funded with Life Insurance)

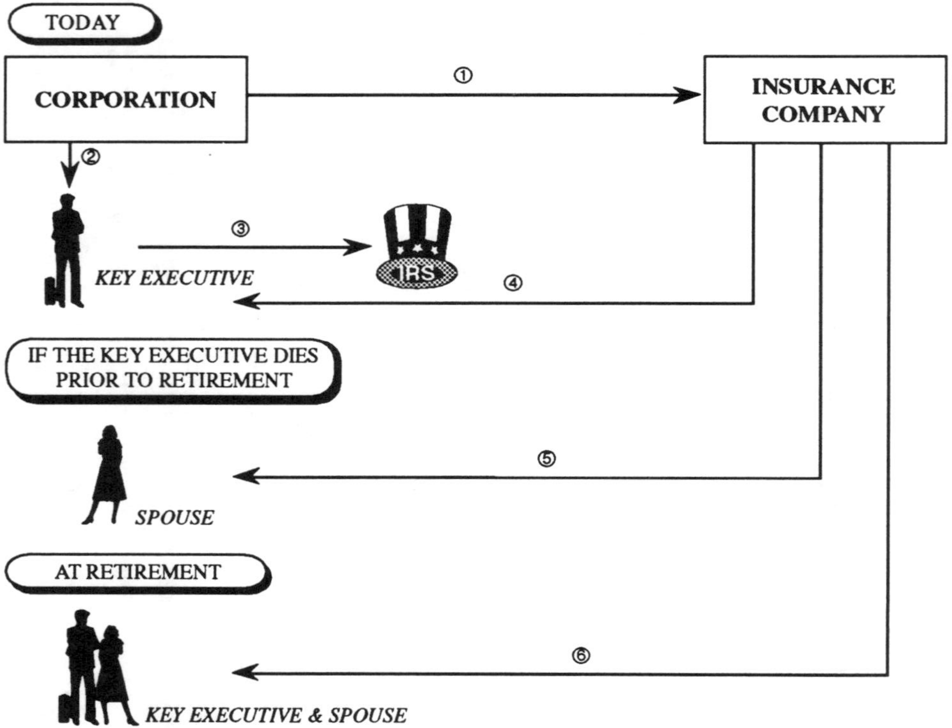

① The corporation pays the annual premium and deducts it.

② The key executive reports the premium as taxable income.

③ The executive pays tax on the premium.

④ The cash value is reflected as an asset on the executive's personal financial statement.

⑤ If the executive dies prior to retirement, the spouse receives the death benefit.

⑥ Assuming the executive lives until retirement, the policy is then used to provide additional retirement income.

☞ CHAPTER 5 ☜

❑

Selective Compensation Planning

If you own your own business, or are a key executive or manager, selective compensation plans are additional ways to create a fortune for yourself and your family.

❑ EXECUTIVE BONUS PLAN

Let's take a look at the diagram on Page 42. The corporation pays the premium on a policy of which the key executive is the owner. This is treated as a bonus to the executive and is deductible by the corporation and taxable to the executive. The executive's cost is the tax on the bonus. The executive is the owner of the policy, and his family or a trust for his family is the beneficiary. Assuming the executive lives until retirement, he then supplements his retirement income by withdrawing money from the cash value. The chart on Page 44 shows the numbers for such a plan.

Key Executive Bonus Plan Summary for Robert Sample (Age 35)

Funded with Life Insurance

Annual Bonus/Premium: $10,000

End of Year	Age	Annual Bonus/ Premium	Executive's Tax Cost @ 40%	Executive's Cumulative Cost	Cash Value	Death Benefit
1	36	$10,000	$4,000	$4,000	$5,823	$1,000,000
5	40	10,000	4,000	20,000	44,767	1,000,000
10	45	10,000	4,000	40,000	117,489	1,000,000
20	55	10,000	4,000	80,000	382,325	1,000,000
30	65	10,000	4,000	120,000	895,934	1,485,982

Summary Assuming Death at Age 85

- ❑ Average Annual Retirement Income (Age 65-85) $54,920

- ❑ Total Retirement Income (Age 65-85) $1,098,400
- ❑ Death Benefit Paid to Family (Age 85) 1,614,872
- ❑ **Total Benefits $2,713,272**

- ❑ Executive's Cost (40% Tax Bracket) $120,000
- ❑ Corporate Cost (40% Tax Bracket) 180,000
- ❑ **Total Cost $300,000**

These figures are based on current assumptions and are not guaranteed.

Group Term vs. Executive Bonus

$1,000,000 (AGE 35)

		PLAN A – GROUP TERM				PLAN B – EXECUTIVE BONUS			
Years	Ages	Annual Taxable Income	Annual Tax Cost at 40%	Cum. Tax Cost	Cash Value	Annual Taxable Income	Annual Tax Cost at 40%	Cum. Tax Cost	Cash Value
1-5	35-39	$1,320	$528	$2,640	$0	$5,000	$2,000	$10,000	$16,187
6-10	40-44	2,040	816	6,720	0	5,000	2,000	20,000	45,782
11-15	45-49	3,480	1,392	13,680	0	5,000	2,000	30,000	87,769
16-20	50-54	5,760	2,304	25,200	0	5,000	2,000	40,000	143,417
21-25	55-59	9,000	3,600	43,200	0	5,000	2,000	50,000	214,761
26-30	60-64	14,040	5,616	71,280	0	5,000	2,000	60,000	304,859

SUMMARY AT AGE 65	PLAN A	PLAN B
EXECUTIVE'S TOTAL TAX COST (AGE 35-65)	$71,280	$60,000
ONGOING INSURANCE	0	1,000,000
TOTAL CASH VALUE	0	304,859

The executive already has $50,000 of group term. This illustration compares plans for an additional $1,000,000.

These figures are based on current assumptions and are not guaranteed.

Which Plan Do You Prefer?

Split-Dollar Life Insurance Overview

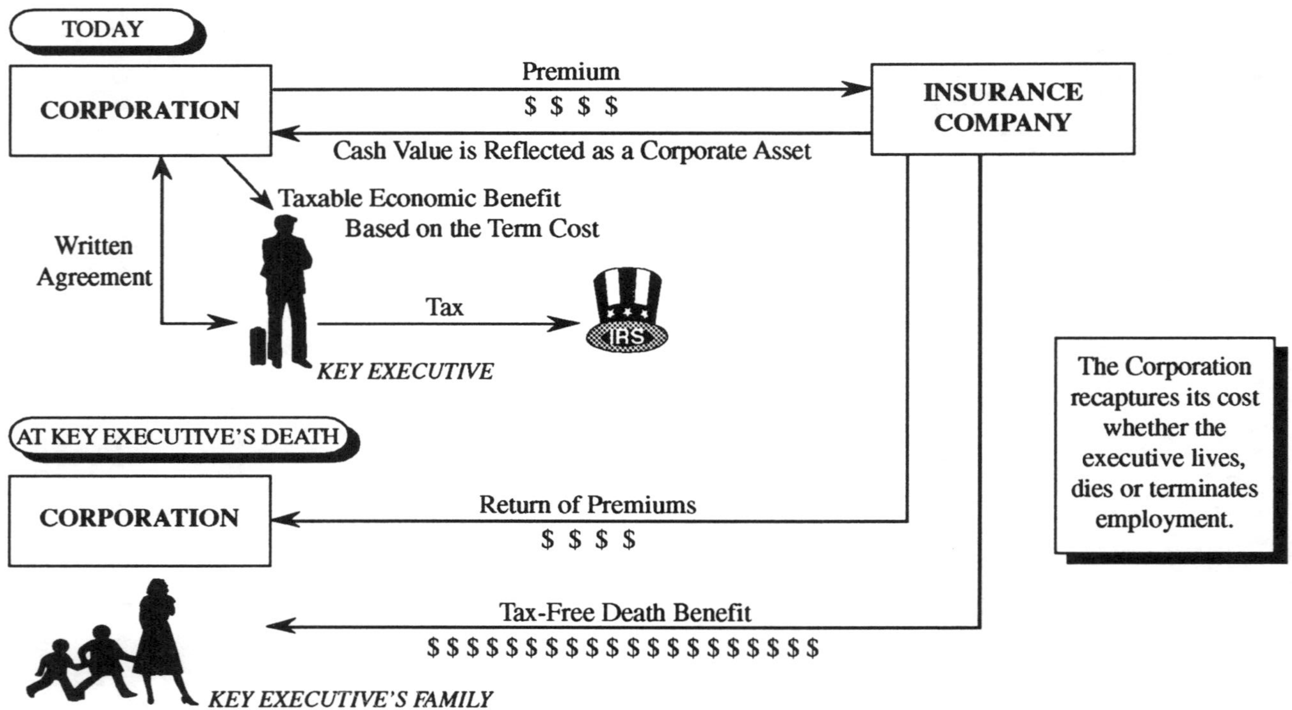

On Page 45, the chart shows clearly why an executive bonus plan is an attractive option when compared to group term insurance.

❑ SPLIT DOLLAR

Now, let's look at the diagram on Page 46. Split dollar is basically a joint venture between the corporation and a key executive wherein the corporation pays the premium on a policy. The corporation recaptures its payments from the cash value or from the death benefit when the executive dies. The executive's cost is that he pays tax on the term cost for the insurance. Would you rather pay the term premium or the tax on the term premium? The answer is obvious, isn't it? Additionally, the cash value can be used to pay supplemental retirement benefits to the executive. The "Men's Wearhouse" article on Page 50 gives an overview of a split-dollar plan used in an estate planning situation.

Another variation of split dollar is reverse split dollar where the corporation rents the insurance from the executive who owns the cash value of the policy. It is basically having someone else pay for the insurance while you get the cash value.

Supplemental Executive Retirement Plan (SERP)

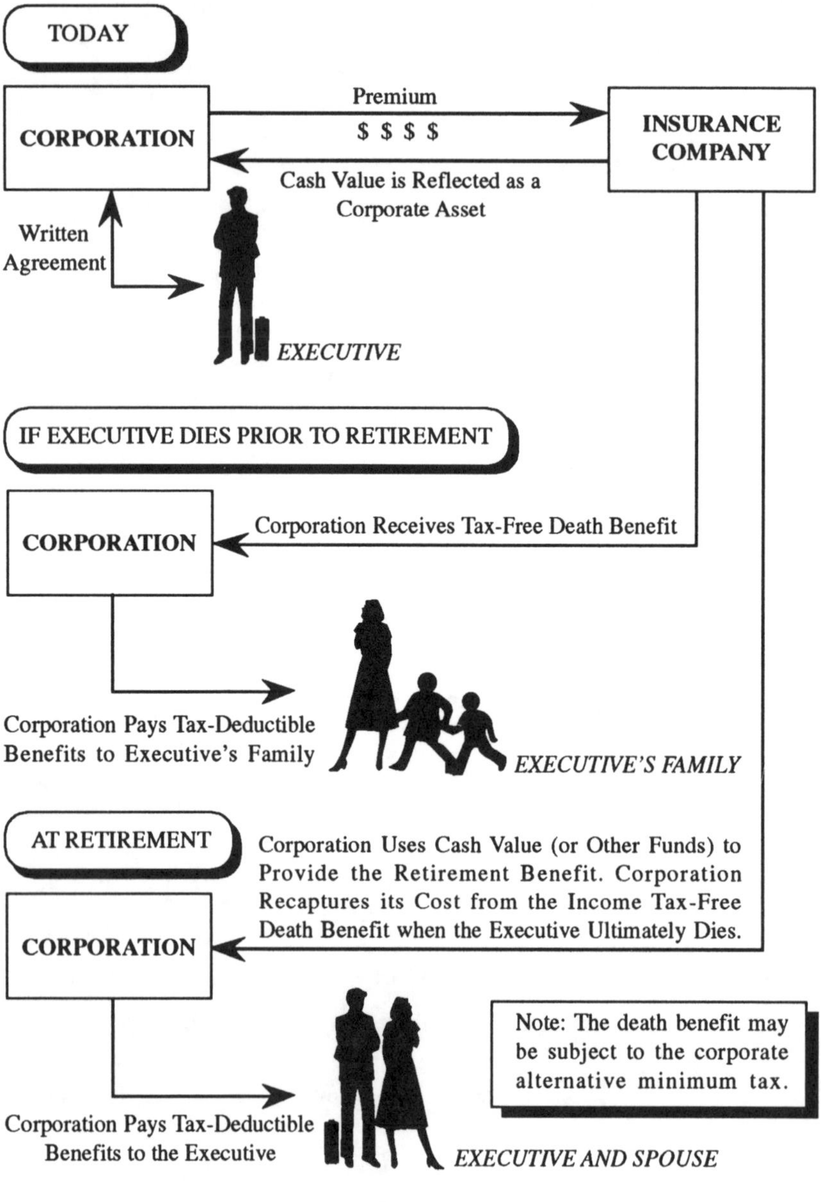

❑ SUPPLEMENTAL EXECUTIVE RETIREMENT PLAN (SERP)

Let's look at the diagram on Page 48. The corporation is the owner and beneficiary of the policy on the key executive. If the executive dies prior to retirement, the corporation uses a portion of the death benefit to pay salary continuation to the executive's family. Assuming the executive lives until retirement, the company pays substantial retirement benefits to the executive, using the cash value or other corporate cash assets, and then recaptures its costs from the policy when the executive dies.

The number of variations of these plans are virtually unlimited.

THE MEN'S WEARHOUSE

Split-Dollar Life Insurance Agreement

The George Zimmer 1988 Living Trust is presently the owner of 2,730,470 shares of the Company's Common Stock. The Company has been advised that on the demise of George Zimmer, his estate may be required to publicly sell all or substantially all of such shares to satisfy estate tax obligations. The public sale of such number of shares in all probability would destabilize the market for the Company's publicly traded stock.

Accordingly, in November 1994, an agreement was entered into (commonly known as a split-dollar life insurance agreement) under the terms of which the Company will make advances of a portion of the premiums for certain life insurance policies on the life of George Zimmer with an aggregate face value of $16,500,000 purchased by a trust established by Mr. Zimmer. To secure the repayment of the advances, the trust has assigned the policies to the Company as collateral.

This information was included in the
1995 Proxy Statement for The Men's Wearhouse, Inc.

☞ CHAPTER 6 ☜

How Much Life Insurance Should You Buy?

There are essentially two schools of thought on how to determine the amount of life insurance you should acquire:

- ❑ Buy what you need to solve specific problems
- ❑ Buy all you can get

Both approaches are valid. Let's examine them.

❑ THE "BUY WHAT YOU NEED TO SOLVE SPECIFIC PROBLEMS" APPROACH

A good rule of thumb for how much insurance to buy is ten times current income which would provide enough income to enable your family to remain in the world which you have created together. To this amount, you could then add other capital needs and then subtract the income producing capital now available. This approach is shown in the worksheet on Page 52.

How Much Money Will Your Family Need When You Die?

	EXAMPLE	YOUR FAMILY
Current Income	$200,000	
Family Income Goal	100,000	
Capital Required @ 5%	2,000,000	
Other Capital Needs *	500,000	
Total Capital Needed	2,500,000	
Income-Producing Capital Available	1,500,000	
Additional Capital Needed	1,000,000	

* *Education fund, mortgage payoff, transition fund, emergency cash cushion, key management loss, final expenses, estate taxes and related costs, etc.*

Based on your situation, you and your agent should be able to identify the specific problems and fill in the numbers in the following section:

Personal Planning

Problem	Dollars Needed
❑ Income Continuation	$ __________
❑ Pay Off Liabilities	__________
❑ Education Fund	__________
❑ Emergency Cash Cushion	__________
❑ Special Bequests	__________
❑ Charitable Bequests	__________
❑ Estate Tax Funding	__________
Total Personal Needs	__________

Business Planning

❑ Buy & Sell Funding	__________
❑ Key Management Loss	__________
❑ Pay Off Loans	__________
❑ Salary Continuation	__________
❑ Selective Compensation Plans	__________
Total Business Needs	__________
Total Personal and Business Needs	__________

How Much Are Your Tomorrows Worth?

- ❑ If you knew you were going to die tomorrow, how much insurance would you buy today? $ ________

- ❑ If you had been killed in a car accident last week, and someone else had been responsible for your death, how much money would your family sue the responsible party for? $ ________

- ❑ If you had been killed in a car accident last week, and you had been responsible, how much money would you want your family to receive? $ ________

- ❑ If you had died of cancer last week, how much money would you want your family to receive? $ ________

- ❑ How much are your tomorrows worth? What is your Potential Earning Power (PEP)? $ ________

- ❑ How much insurance is there on your life? $ ________

How Much Your Tomorrows Are Worth

WHAT IS YOUR POTENTIAL EARNING POWER?

YEARS TO RETIRE-MENT	AVERAGE ANNUAL EARNINGS TO RETIREMENT				
	$25,000	**$50,000**	**$75,000**	**$100,000**	**$200,000**
	YOUR TOMORROWS ARE WORTH				
40	$1,000,000	$2,000,000	$3,000,000	$4,000,000	$8,000,000
35	875,000	1,750,000	2,625,000	3,500,000	7,000,000
30	750,000	1,500,000	2,250,000	3,000,000	6,000,000
25	625,000	1,250,000	1,875,000	2,500,000	5,000,000
20	500,000	1,000,000	1,500,000	2,000,000	4,000,000
15	375,000	750,000	1,125,000	1,500,000	3,000,000
10	250,000	500,000	750,000	1,000,000	2,000,000

Your Estimated Average Annual Earnings to Retirement $________

Years to Retirement at Age ______ x________

Your Tomorrows Are Worth **$**________

If You Were Killed in a Car Accident, and Someone Else was Responsible, How Much Would Your Family Sue For? $________

How Much Life Insurance is there on Your Life? $________

How Much Life Insurance Can You Buy?

These figures represent how much life insurance one major company will issue without further substantiation. For example, if you are now 35 and are earning $100,000 annually, $1,300,000 would be the maximum insurance protection available (including insurance in force) for your family. If you were killed in a car accident, and someone else were responsible for your death, an attorney representing your family would undoubtedly sue the responsible party for a lot more than that. In that context, it makes sense to insure your life for as much as possible, wouldn't you agree? Why not get all the insurance you can get?

AGE	INCOME MULTIPLIER
20	16
25	15
30	14
35	13
40	12
45	11
50	9
55	8
60	6
65	4

Age Now	________
Annual Income	$ ________
Income Multiplier	________
Maximum Insurance Protection	$ ________
Minus Insurance You Now Have	– ________
Additional Insurance	$ ________

❑ THE "BUY ALL YOU CAN GET" APPROACH

How much are your tomorrows worth? Use the worksheets on Pages 54 and 55 to determine your Potential Earning Power.

If you knew you were going to die tomorrow, how much life insurance would you buy today? Most people, when asked that question, say they would buy all they can get. Of course, by the time you know when you are going to die, it is already too late to buy any.

If you died in a car accident last week, and someone else had been responsible for your death, how much would an attorney representing your family sue the responsible party for? All they could get!

The most valuable asset you own is your Potential Earning Power (PEP), which some refer to as your human life value. For example, if you were now age 35 and earning $100,000 annually, over the next 30 years until age 65, your potential earning power would be $3,000,000. This disregards any increases in earnings. Wouldn't it make sense for your family, if you are the primary breadwinner, to insure you for as much as possible?

How much life insurance can you get according to a life insurance company? Let's have a look at the worksheet on Page 56. Using our example, this individual could get $100,000 multiplied by 13, or $1,300,000, at age 35.

Almost everyone insures their home, their cars, their furniture, and their jewelry for as much as possible. Doesn't it make sense to do the same thing when it comes to life insurance?

> *If you could insure one, but not both,*
> *which would you insure . . .*
> *the golden eggs or the goose?*

❑ FORESIGHT

My experience has been that successful people keep buying more and more life insurance. Not only do their needs increase, but they also increasingly recognize their value and responsibility to others.

It takes foresight to buy insurance in the first place, because you are buying something which hopefully will not be needed for years. It takes even greater foresight and insight to understand that the best time to buy is now, and that you should buy as much as you possibly can.

Buying as much life insurance as you possibly can means that you have an understanding of the power of life insurance as being a tremendous asset to own. Life insurance can help you create a fortune for your family if you have not had time. It can help you create a fortune for retirement to supplement your other investments, and it can help you save your fortune from the devastation of estate taxes and related costs. Life insurance is the cornerstone for building a firm foundation for your family's financial future.

Is Life Insurance a Good Investment?

The best investment is the one that provides you with the most money when you need it the most.

Using that common-sense criterion,
life insurance is a pretty good investment,
wouldn't you agree?

THE FIRST LAW OF INSURANCE

Insure First

That Which You Can

Least Afford To Lose

Your Potential

Earning Power

☞ CHAPTER 7 ☜

What Type of Insurance Should You Buy and How Much Will it Cost?

There are basically two types of insurance for our purposes:

- ❑ Term Insurance
- ❑ Cash Value Insurance

Term insurance builds no equity or cash value. All you get is the insurance protection. When you stop paying, term insurance terminates and you will have paid a lot for nothing.

Accidental death insurance and flight insurance are indications that your overall insurance program is inadequate. Under no circumstances should you buy either. Your family needs adequate protection regardless of how you die.

Summary Of Insurance Options
For Robert Sample

$1,000,000 (AGE 35)		**PLAN A**	**PLAN B**	**PLAN C**
YEAR	AGE	ANNUAL PREMIUM		
1	36	$614	$5,000	$10,000
5	40	764	5,000	10,000
10	45	1,184	5,000	10,000
20	55	2,544	5,000	10,000
30	65	9,004	5,000	10,000
Total Premiums (Age 35-65)		**$79,380**	**$150,000**	**$300,000**
SUMMARY OF OPTIONS AT AGE 65				
❑ Insurance		0*	$1,000,000	$1,571,495
❑ Cash Value		0	304,859	947,499
❑ Annual Lifetime Income		0	23,108	71,819

These figures are based on current assumptions and are not guaranteed.

* Term insurance terminates when you stop paying.

PLAN A: Term Insurance
PLAN B: Cash Value Insurance
PLAN C: Cash Value Insurance

If you were now age 65 and were looking back, which plan would you prefer to have purchased at age 35?

Which Plan Do You Prefer?

Cash value insurance includes whole life, universal life, variable life, and the many combinations and blends thereof.

Let's take a look at the chart on Page 62. This summarizes about twelve pages of computer printouts. It compares options for $1,000,000 of insurance starting at age 35. Plan A is term insurance and starts out with a premium of only $614 the first year, but it is like a stairway to nowhere. It keeps going up and up and up until at age 65, the premium for that year alone is about $9,000. The total premiums paid for term insurance from age 35 to age 65 would be almost $80,000.

Let's compare those numbers with Plans B and C, which are cash value policies. With Plan B, you will have paid $150,000 rather than $80,000. For an additional $70,000, you would have $1,000,000 of ongoing insurance, or about $300,000 in cash value, or a lifetime annual income of about $23,000.

With Plan C, the annual premium is $10,000. At age 65, you would have paid $300,000. You would have over $1,500,000 of ongoing insurance, or almost $950,000 in cash value, or a lifetime annual income of about $71,000.

Which Plan Do You Prefer?

This Plan ABC comparison approach makes it easy to see what your options are. You can basically tailor the options to match your goals and budget.

As you can see from the chart, term insurance is incredibly cheap. You can easily afford adequate insurance to protect your family and your business.

So, if term insurance is so cheap, why doesn't everyone just buy term?

Term insurance is cheap because the insurance company does not expect to have to pay. The majority of people do not die before age 65. About 20% of people die before age 65, which means about 80% die after age 65.

With term insurance, you are spending money. With cash value insurance, you are saving money. Most people would rather own than rent. You are renting term insurance. You own cash value insurance. It builds equity in the form of cash value.

❑ SHOULD YOU BUY TERM INSURANCE AND INVEST THE DIFFERENCE?

Most of the financial press would advise you to buy term insurance and invest the difference yourself. The "difference" referred to is the annual premium difference between what a term policy costs and what a cash value policy costs. If you examine the numbers, I think you will agree that over the long haul, cash value insurance makes the most sense for most people.

Let's take a look at the chart below. In order to facilitate the comparison, we have invented a term policy which has a level premium of only $1,000 per year for $1,000,000 of insurance starting at age 35. The total premiums paid for this policy from age 35 to 65 would be only $30,000. (Note: You can't buy this policy in the marketplace; it is a hypothetical plan which is much cheaper over the long haul than any term policy available.)

Term vs. Cash Value Comparison

$1,000,000 (AGE 35)	PLAN A	PLAN B	PLAN C	PLAN D
Annual Premium (Age 35-65)	$1,000	$5,000	$10,000	$20,000
SUMMARY AT AGE 65				
Total Premiums (Age 35-65)	$30,000	$150,000	$300,000	$600,000
Ongoing Insurance	0	1,000,000	1,571,495	2,956,894
Cash Value	0	304,859	947,499	1,783,036
Annual Compound Rate of Return on Additional Premium (Compared to Plan A)	0	5.48%	7.21%	6.60%

These figures are based on current assumptions and are not guaranteed.

Which Plan Do You Prefer?

Using an HP-12C calculator, we have determined that the rate of return on the $4,000 annual premium difference (Plan B vs. Plan A) would be 5.48% net-after-taxes. Comparing Plan A with Plan C, the additional premium, $9,000, would be growing at a rate of 7.21% net-after-taxes. In a 30% marginal income tax bracket (state and federal combined), that is equivalent to better than 10% pre-tax.

If you could get 10% on certificates of deposit, how much money would you want to put in the stock market or in mutual funds?

If you were investing the annual premium difference yourself, what would happen if you were disabled? How long would you be able to continue investing the difference? With the cash value insurance, we have included the waiver of premium benefit. This means that if you were disabled, after six months of disability, the premium would be waived, and the cash value would continue to grow as if the premiums were being paid. This benefit separates cash value insurance from all other investments.

If you feel that you would be getting too low a rate of return on cash value insurance, even after running through the numbers as we have just done, it is important to realize that most insurance companies now have a variable life insurance product which gives you the option of having your money invested in what are basically mutual funds. In many instances, the insurance companies have formed strategic alliances with mutual funds so that the mutual funds are managing the money for the insurance company. You can choose to have your money invested in an index fund which approximates the S&P 500, an aggressive growth fund, a total return fund, or whatever you prefer.

❑ THE TAX ASPECTS OF LIFE INSURANCE

Let's take a quick look at the tax aspects of life insurance. When you are purchasing life insurance personally, the premium is not deductible. However, the cash value accumulates on a tax-deferred basis and you can borrow the cash value out of the policy without paying taxes. The death benefit will in almost all situations be income-tax free.

❑ CONCLUSION

Ask your agent to provide you with a comparison of term and cash value insurance policies. This should greatly facilitate your decision-making. It will enable you to determine the type of insurance that you want to buy, and it will enable you to determine how much you want to pay for it. Remember, with term insurance you are spending money, while with cash value insurance, you are saving money.

When you stop paying for term insurance, term insurance terminates. You will have paid a lot for nothing.

> *Life is a marathon . . . not a sprint.*
> *Term insurance is built for the sprint.*
> *Cash value insurance is built*
> *for the marathon.*

Alphabet Soup

When is an A+ not an A+? Possibly when it comes to rating the financial condition of an insurance company. To most of us, A+ sounds like a pretty good grade, but when it comes to rating insurance companies, it depends upon who is doing the rating. This chart makes it possible to determine how one rating compares with another from the standpoint of the level of the rating. For example, A+ is a second level rating from A.M. Best, but it is the top level rating from Weiss Research. Because ratings are on the same level does not make them equivalent, as the definitions vary considerably among the rating services. In other words, there is no way to directly compare ratings. Is it any wonder that people are confused? We recommend that you review the ratings from A.M. Best Company and two other rating services.

	RATINGS				
RANKING LEVEL	A.M. BEST COMPANY	STANDARD & POOR'S	MOODY'S	DUFF & PHELPS	WEISS RESEARCH
1	A++	AAA	Aaa	AAA	A+
2	A+	AA+	Aa1	AA+	A
3	A	AA	Aa2	AA	A-
4	A-	AA-	Aa3	AA-	B+
5	B++	A+	A1	A+	B
6	B+	A	A2	A	B-
7	B	A-	A3	A-	C+
8	B-	BBB+	Baa1	BBB+	C
9	C++	BBB	Baa2	BBB	C-
10	C+	BBB-	Baa3	BBB-	D+
11	C	BB+	Ba1	BB+	D
12	C-	BB	Ba2	BB	D-
13	D	BB-	Ba3	BB-	E+
14	E	B+	B1	B+	E
15	F	B	B2	B	F
16		B-	B3	B-	
17		CCC	Caa	CCC+	
18		R	Ca	CCC	
19			C	CCC-	

☞ CHAPTER 8 ☜

From Whom Should You Buy?

❑ HOW DO YOU SELECT A COMPANY?

There are more than 2,000 life insurance companies doing business in the United States. How do you choose one? If you have been contacted by an agent, he or she undoubtedly does most of his or her business with a relatively limited number of companies.

There are several organizations which rate insurance companies with regard to their financial strength and claims paying ability. The chart entitled "Alphabet Soup" on Page 68 shows the ratings used by these organizations. In selecting an insurance company, I suggest that you stick to companies having ratings which are in the shaded area on the chart. This is a rather arbitrary determination, but there are a lot of companies that will qualify. For your own peace of mind, you may only want to do business with companies falling within the top two ranking levels. On the other hand, an agent may be able to make an extremely strong case as to why you should do business with a company falling outside of these guidelines.

Where do you get the ratings information? You should be able to get them in your local library if you want to do some research on your own, or your agent can provide them to you for the companies you are considering.

Your agent should also be able to provide you with reports from the A.M. Best Company which show the projections and actual results over twenty years where companies are compared side by side. In an increasingly competitive industry, it is important to know how a company has done in terms of delivering actual results as compared to other companies. Over the years, it seems that the same companies keep repeating as the leaders in performance.

❑ HOW DO YOU SELECT AN AGENT?

If an agent has been referred to you by a friend or business associate, you should ask them how long they have been working with the agent and how pleased they are with the work the agent has done for them. If you are actively seeking an agent on your own, I recommend that you check with your friends and find someone who is extremely happy with the job done by their agent. Then contact that agent.

If the agent contacted you direct, you may want to get the names of some of his or her clients and check with them.

One of the most important factors to take into consideration is your gut reaction to someone. If you sense that you don't like them or that you can't trust them, don't work with them.

In terms of credentials, you can look for an agent who is a Chartered Life Underwriter (CLU) or a Chartered Financial Consultant (ChFC), and a member of the Million Dollar Round Table (MDRT). There are many top agents who march to the tune of a different drummer, so the fact that an agent is none of these should not be a deterrent to working with them if you feel comfortable.

If an agent is new in the business, this should not be a deterrent to working with them if your gut reaction is that the agent is trustworthy and knowledgeable. Looking back to 1969, my first year in the insurance business, I would hate to think that people would not have worked with me just because I was new both to the business and to the San Francisco Bay Area. Once I had my first client, I had someone that other people could check with to determine the quality of my work. Plus, I had exceptionally good training.

Again, in selecting an agent with whom to work, I cannot overemphasize the importance of trusting your gut reaction. The relationship that you will have with your insurance agent hopefully will be a lifelong relationship. It should be with someone with whom you feel comfortable and it should ultimately be a relationship where you view the agent as a trusted advisor . . . not just as a salesperson.

❑ THE WIMP FACTOR

You do not want a wimp for a life insurance agent! Your family cannot afford for you to have a wimp for an insurance agent. You deserve an agent who will tell you what you need to hear . . . not just what you would like to hear. Your agent is your financial conscience.

❑ WHO SHOULD BE INVOLVED IN YOUR MEETINGS?

The decision makers should be present. Both the husband and the wife should be involved in the meetings with the agent. In some homes, one spouse may be primarily responsible for making the financial decisions. Even if that is the case, both spouses should take part in the planning process, because the entire family is going to be impacted by what the planning accomplishes.

❑ WHEN SHOULD YOU MEET?

When do you meet with your doctor, your dentist, your attorney, or your accountant? You probably make appointments during the day to see these people. Next to your physical health, I cannot imagine anything more important than your family's financial health. I suggest you meet with your agent at his or her office during normal business hours if at all possible.

❑ WHAT SHOULD YOU EXPECT FROM YOUR AGENT?

In your relationship with your agent, what are the factors that constitute value from your perspective?

❑ Rapport	❑ Solutions	❑ Communication
❑ Price	❑ Quality	❑ Service
❑ Cost	❑ Integrity	❑ Trust
❑ Benefits	❑ Follow-through	❑ Peace of Mind
❑ Ideas	❑ Performance	❑ The Relationship

Those factors that are important to you will differ from those that are important to others.

LIFE INSURANCE

"The advantage of life insurance as an investment is that you make one purchase and then forget about it except for the annual premiums you pay. Insurance protects you from yourself; it allows the cash value to accumulate without your being able to spend it. In addition to an investment, you also have protection for your family in the event of your death."

CHRISTINA ROBERTSON
Author of *A Woman's Guide to Divorce and Decision Making*

CHAPTER 9

When Should You Buy?

> *The best time to buy is now . . .*
> *before it's too late.*

NOW! It is that simple. If you wait, your health might change. You might have the ultimate health change. You might die. Waiting means your age will increase which means the cost will increase, and the benefits will decrease. There is no advantage to be gained by waiting.

What should you do if you have not decided whether you want term insurance or cash value insurance? Apply now for the term insurance, and then convert it later to cash value insurance. Get the insurance in force.

The good news is that there is a built-in "thinking it over" period in the process. Generally speaking, it will take 4-8 weeks or more to determine if you qualify for the insurance. From the time you actually receive the policy from your agent, you have another ten days during which you can still get your money back.

Most people have a natural desire to want to think things over. Procrastination is one of the biggest challenges most of us face on an ongoing basis in our lives. Why should it be any different when it comes to making decisions regarding life insurance? It's only normal not to want to discuss your own death.

It is important that you realize your agent is acting in your best interest by getting you to take action as soon as possible. Companies have different rules regarding taking a check and giving you a conditional receipt when you apply for insurance. Most companies' conditional receipts state that you will be covered as of the time the agent has a check and you have completed the required medical examination and tests, assuming you are insurable at standard rates. Some companies will insure you even though it may not be at the standard rate.

If the company's rules permit the agent's giving you a conditional receipt for the amount of insurance for which you are applying, I heartily recommend that you give your agent a check (made payable to the insurance company) and transfer the risk from yourself and your family to the insurance company.

❑ YOUR HEALTH

You should be aware that your own doctor may view your health from a totally different perspective than how an insurance company views it. Your doctor is viewing it in terms of the present and a few years into the future. An insurance company is viewing it in terms of your life expectancy. From an insurance company's viewpoint, your dying in ten years rather than thirty or forty can make a big difference in its results if it is wrong on a large number of lives.

❑ THE BOTTOM LINE

The bottom line is that you should acquire the maximum amount of insurance you are willing to buy as soon as possible. The best time is now.

> *You have the opportunity of a lifetime right now to create and save a fortune using life insurance. Why wait?*

Should You Insure Your Spouse?

WHEN A SPOUSE DIES, THERE IS A TREMENDOUS *EMOTIONAL* LOSS. OFTEN OVERLOOKED IS THE POTENTIAL *ECONOMIC* LOSS WHICH CAN MAKE THE EMOTIONAL LOSS EVEN WORSE.

	Potential Cost	**Years**	**Total Cost**
Final Expenses (Funeral, Hospital and Medical Expenses)	$20,000	–	$20,000
Estate and Inheritance Taxes, Probate Fees, Attorney, CPA	10,000	–	10,000
Lost Income (if Spouse was Producing Income)	50,000	5	250,000
Cost of Cook, Housekeeper, Sitter, Shopper, Seamstress, Nurse, Chauffeur, Laundress, etc.	20,000	5	100,000
Increase in Income Taxes (Head of Household vs. Joint)	2,000±	5	10,000
Total Potential Cost			**$390,000**

NOTE: These figures do not take into account the impact the spouse's death may have on the survivor's ability to perform at a high level. The surviving spouse's earning potential may be impaired for some time.

☞ CHAPTER 10 ☜

☐

Should You Insure Your Spouse?

If your spouse were to die, wouldn't there be a tremendous emotional loss? Would you be able to function as you normally do, or would you be walking around in a fog for some period of time? If you work for someone else, would you be as effective at work as you normally are? If you work for yourself, would you just be going through the motions but not accomplishing much?

The worksheet on Page 78 will help you put a price tag on the economic loss associated with the death of a spouse, but it is important to recognize that the largest economic loss may be associated with your own inability to produce at the same level that you were prior to your spouse's death.

It's easy to understand the economic impact with regard to the loss of earned income. You can also identify the cost of replacing the services your spouse provided at home. What's tougher to identify is the economic impact that their loss will have on your own income.

You may have to take several months off to care for your children, find a housekeeper, and deal with your own grief. If there is no life insurance, you may have to take a second job in order to just make ends meet. What would these scenarios, or others, cost you personally? What is the potential economic loss?

CHAPTER 11

Should You Buy Insurance on Your Children or Grandchildren?

Most members of the financial press would advise you against buying life insurance on your children or grandchildren. As you might expect, I totally disagree.

You would be buying life insurance on your children from two perspectives. First you would buy it to offset the financial impact that a child's death would have on you. The death of a child often means that the parent is incapable of performing productively for quite some time. They may go to work, but they are only going through the motions. Therefore, the impact would probably be more in the loss of your own income than in terms of the funeral and miscellaneous costs associated with the child's death.

The Advantages of an Early Start

Initial Life Insurance	**$1,000,000**			
Starting Age	**5**	**15**	**25**	**35**
Annual Premium	$6,520	$8,960	$12,400	$19,060
Total Premiums to Age 65	391,200	448,000	496,000	571,800
Cash Value at Age 65	7,092,529	4,379,475	2,727,271	1,792,527
Gain	6,701,329	3,931,475	2,231,271	1,220,727
Ongoing Insurance at Age 65	11,761,877	7,262,691	4,522,767	2,972,633

These figures are based on current assumptions and are not guaranteed.

IF YOU WAIT

- ❑ Your child may die without the insurance.
- ❑ Your child's health may change.
- ❑ The cost increases.
- ❑ The benefits decrease.
- ❑ Term insurance bought as an interim measure only adds to the cost of waiting.
- ❑ The best time to buy is now!

Why not start now?

WHY WAIT?

More importantly, I am recommending that you buy insurance for your children as a way of giving them a head start in their financial lives. Right now, hopefully your children are in good health and they are not smoking. They are not involved in drugs. They haven't become involved in bungee jumping or other death defying avocations. They haven't chosen a career that an insurance company might find risky.

Right now, they can probably acquire life insurance at a better rate than will ever be available to them again.

It is important to reemphasize the role life insurance plays in terms of creating a fortune. The sooner you start, the sooner you have the power of compound interest working for you, or in this case, for your children.

If you wait, your children's health might change or they might die. Waiting means the cost will increase, and the benefits will decrease. See *The Advantages of an Early Start* on Page 82.

Capital Requirements Analysis

FOR BOB AND JANE SMITH

		BOB	JANE
Age Now		30	28
Current Income		$60,000	$20,000
Years to Retirement at Bob's Age 65		35	35
Potential Earning Power (Current Income x Years to Retirement)		$2,100,000	$700,000
CAPITAL REQUIREMENTS			
First to Die		Bob	Jane
Income Goal for Family		$40,000	$40,000
Income Available (Surviving Spouse's Income)		20,000	60,000
Income Shortage		20,000	–
Capital Required @ 5% to Generate $20,000 Annually	(A)	**400,000**	–
Misc. Capital Requirements			
Pay Off Mortgage		100,000	100,000
Other Liabilities		20,000	20,000
Cash Cushion & Transition Fund		50,000	50,000
Emergency Fund		40,000	40,000
Education Fund ($20,000 x 4 Years x 2 Children)		160,000	160,000
Final Expenses		10,000	10,000
Income Taxes, Legal, Accounting, Etc.		5,000	5,000
Estate Taxes & Related Costs		–	–
Total Misc. Capital Requirements	(B)	**385,000**	**385,000**
TOTAL CAPITAL REQUIRED (A + B)	(C)	**$785,000**	**$385,000**
CAPITAL NOW AVAILABLE			
Group Life Insurance		120,000	–
Personal Life Insurance		50,000	–
Other Income–Producing Assets		130,000	130,000
TOTAL CAPITAL NOW AVAILABLE	(D)	**300,000**	**130,000**
ADDITIONAL CAPITAL REQUIRED (C – D)	(E)	**$485,000**	**$255,000**

☞ CHAPTER 12 ☜

Dual-Income Couples

The worksheet on Page 84 will help you and your agent determine how much life insurance you need. Or, perhaps you should just purchase as much as you can get rather than limiting the amount as a result of this analysis.

As we have presented the question before,

> *If you knew you were going to die tomorrow, how much life insurance would you buy today?*

Most people say that they would buy as much as they could get. Why not do that?

Dual-income couples who are not married should note that if marriage is an option, it would potentially save them a lot of money in terms of estate taxes. When married, the first spouse can leave everything to the surviving spouse without estate taxes. That is not the case with a couple who are not married.

How Much Disability Insurance Do I Need?

ANNUAL LIVING EXPENSES	Example	Your Family
Housing	$ 20,000	$
Phone and Utilities	3,000	
Food	12,000	
Clothing	6,000	
Transportation	6,000	
Entertainment	3,000	
Education	20,000	
Medical, Personal Care	6,000	
Life Insurance	2,000	
Spouse's Job-Related Expenses	1,500	
Other Expenses	–	
TOTAL ANNUAL LIVING EXPENSES	**$ 79,500**	**$**
INCOME DURING DISABILITY		
Spouse's After-Tax Income	10,000	
Investment Income	0	
Group Disability Income	0	
Individual Disability Income	0	
Other Income	0	
TOTAL ANNUAL INCOME	**$ 10,000**	**$**
ANNUAL INCOME SHORTAGE	**$ 69,500**	**$**

☞ CHAPTER 13 ☜

How Much Disability Income Insurance Do You Need?

If you were unable to work as a result of sickness or accident, how long would you continue receiving income from your job? How long would your savings last?

One year of disability could result in the loss of ten years' savings!

Think about it. Just one year of disability could mean the loss of ten years' savings. Amazing, isn't it?

While statistics don't matter when it comes to individuals, the probability of disability prior to age 65 is higher than the probability of death. The bottom line is you cannot afford to not have disability income insurance unless you are independently wealthy.

Some people can't imagine anything short of death keeping them from working. What about a stroke? What about a back pain so severe that you can only stand for a few minutes at a time?

I purchased my first house from someone who had just retired from his job as a result of having suffered multiple heart attacks over a period of several years. He could no longer afford to live in the home, and he and his wife moved into an apartment.

The worksheet on Page 86 is intended to help you and your agent determine how much disability income insurance you need.

In addition to purchasing the disability income insurance, I also recommend that you add the disability waiver of premium benefit to your life insurance. This means that if you are disabled for six months or more, the insurance company will waive the premium for the duration of the disability and refund the premium paid during the six-month waiting period.

On a cash value policy, the cash value will continue to grow as if the premiums had been paid. If you are systematically investing in mutual funds and are disabled, the mutual fund company is not going to make the investments for you. This is what separates cash value insurance from other investments as an accumulation vehicle.

☞ CHAPTER 14 ☜

Questions and Answers

Q **Why should I buy life insurance?**

A If your death will create an economic loss for your family, your business, your estate, your community, your church or temple, your college or school, or your favorite charity, you probably need some more life insurance. If your death will not result in an economic loss for one of those entities, you might want to ask yourself why.

Q Why should I buy life insurance? **When I am gone . . . that's their problem.**

A Are you saying that because you really mean it . . . or are you saying that just to avoid the purchase of life insurance? You probably don't really mean it. Caring, responsible people just don't think that way.

Q Why should I buy life insurance? **My spouse can work.**

A What if you were killed in a car accident and your spouse were totally disabled? Would you want your spouse's entire future to be totally contingent upon their ability to work?

Q Why should I buy life insurance? **My spouse can remarry.**

A What if you were killed in a car accident and your spouse were totally disabled? Would you want your spouse's entire future to be totally contingent upon their ability to remarry?

Q Why should I buy life insurance? **My spouse can sell the house and move into a smaller one.**

A If your spouse had died a month ago, would you sell your home and move into a smaller one? Of course not!

Q Why should I buy life insurance? **God will take care of my family.**

A Let me tell you a story about a farmer who felt the same way. When he met with an insurance agent, he told the agent that he didn't need any life insurance because God would take care of his family.

Several weeks later, his family is out of town, and there are severe rains which are flooding the community. The waters have risen so high that the farmer has taken refuge on the second floor of his home, since the first floor is underwater. A rowboat nears his home and one of its occupants offers to rescue the farmer. The farmer thanks them but tells them, "God will take care of me." The waters continue to rise so that the farmer has now been forced out on the roof of his home. At this time, a helicopter flies by, and its occupants offer to rescue him. Again the farmer says, "God will take care of me."

The bad news is the farmer drowned in the flood, and his family is now destitute.

One day in heaven, the farmer encounters God who asks how he is. The farmer replies, "I am disappointed in You. I always told everyone that You would take care of me and my family, and You let me down."

To which God responded, "What do you mean by saying that I let you down? I sent an insurance agent, a rowboat, and a helicopter. What more could I have done?"

Q Why should I buy life insurance? **I am single.**

A If there is anyone who is now, or who will be in the future, counting on you for income, you probably need some insurance. The best time to buy is now. Maybe you would like to leave special bequests to a friend, or to your parents, or to brothers and sisters, or to a favorite charity.

Q Why should I buy life insurance now? **I am planning on losing weight and should be able to get a better price then.**

A Get some insurance in force right now. Your health could grow worse or you might die.

Q **What if I have a health problem?** Can I get, and afford to buy, life insurance?

A If life insurance makes sense when you think you are in perfect health, it certainly makes sense when you find out that you aren't. In any event, there are companies which specialize in policies for people who have specific health problems. A good agent will be able to help you in this regard. Get some insurance in force as soon as possible, and then explore more options. Don't wait.

Q **My doctor tells me I am in good health.** The insurance company wants to charge me more because of a specific health condition. Why should I buy the insurance given those facts?

A Your doctor is looking at your health now and for the next few years. The insurance company is looking at you in terms of the next 30-50 years. It is a totally different perspective. Get the insurance now. Then ask your agent to check out other insurance companies.

Q **Why shouldn't I just buy term insurance and invest the difference myself?**

A Life is a marathon . . . not a sprint. Term insurance is built for the sprint. Cash value insurance is built for the marathon. Buying term and investing the difference is like running a marathon. In a marathon, you can be ahead for 26 miles, and if you fall behind in the last few hundred yards, you still lose. It's the same thing with buying term and investing the difference. You can be ahead by buying term and investing the difference for 10 or 15 years, but when you fall behind, you still lose, regardless of how long you were ahead. See Pages 64 and 65 for further explanation.

Q **How much faith should I place in the computer illustrations?**

A It probably makes sense to get additional illustrations that assume lower investment returns. It never hurts to base your planning on more conservative assumptions. Although there are always exceptions, the companies that have been the most competitive in the past seem to be the most competitive consistently.

Q **My insurance agent has recommended an insurance company which I have never heard of.** Should I buy insurance from that company?

A The primary purpose of life insurance is to provide peace of mind. I don't want to be the one to discourage doing business with small companies . . . but the company should be able to pass your sleep test. Of course, some companies which you may not have heard of may, in fact, be extremely big. (Read Chapter 8 on how to select a company.) Ask your agent to show you the company's financial ratings. Ask the agent why he isn't doing business with a company that you have heard of. He should be able to answer your questions to your complete satisfaction or you should not doing business with him.

Q **My stockbroker sells life insurance.** Should I buy from him?

A Do you consider your stockbroker to be an expert when it comes to overall life insurance planning? His or her firm may have an insurance specialist. Otherwise, I would recommend you work with an agent who is a full-time specialist in life insurance planning.

Q **Why should I have to pay interest to borrow my cash value when it is my own money?**

A When you borrow on margin using your stock portfolio as collateral, it works the same way. When you use an equity line of credit, using the equity in your home as collateral, you are doing the same thing. You are basically paying interest to get access to your own money.

Q Why should I buy more life insurance? **If I do, I will be worth more dead than alive.**

A How much are your tomorrows worth? If you are now 35 and earning $100,000 annually, over the next 30 years to age 65, your Potential Earning Power (PEP) is $3,000,000, totally disregarding any increase in earnings. You are worth far more alive than dead!

Q **Won't the need for life insurance decrease as I build an estate?**

A While you may no longer need insurance in order to create a fortune for your family, you may need insurance in order to save a fortune from estate taxes. For most people, the need for insurance is permanent, not temporary.

Q **My attorney and accountant say I don't need life insurance.** Why should I buy any life insurance?

A Is that their professional opinion or personal opinion? Are they going to provide the cash your family will need? Of course not! Will they provide the cash your business will need? Of course not! Are they going to pay the taxes? Of course not!

If you want your estate to go to your children (or grandchildren), life insurance represents the most cost-effective way to pay the estate taxes. See Chapter 3, *How to Save A Fortune Using Life Insurance*, for more details. Sometimes people confuse the goal. They forget that the goal is to get as much as possible to their heirs.

Sometimes they think the goal is to avoid the purchase of life insurance regardless of how cost effective it is.

IF LIFE INSURANCE WERE FREE, HOW MUCH WOULD YOU WANT?

☞ Appendix ☜

Top Ten Money Management Maxims

- ❑ **PLAN.** Look at the big picture. Avoid piecemeal planning.
- ❑ **DIVERSIFY.** Don't put all your eggs in one basket. Don't invest your money with people unless they have a good track record or you can afford to lose the money.
- ❑ **SELLING PLAN.** When you invest, have a selling plan. Anyone can buy something. The pros have a selling plan.
- ❑ **ADVISORS.** Get professional advice . . . but remember that it's your money.
- ❑ **PAY YOURSELF FIRST.** Save first and then spend the rest. Try to save and invest 10% of your gross income. Set aside something systematically each month. Have an emergency cash reserve of 3-6 months' income.
- ❑ **TIME AND MONEY.** Understand the impact of Taxes, Inflation, Mistakes, Emergencies, and compound interest on your money.
- ❑ **HEALTH INSURANCE.** Ensure that you have adequate medical and disability insurance.
- ❑ **LIFE INSURANCE.** Have adequate life insurance to ensure that your family can maintain their current standard of living. When your estate is large, use life insurance to pay the estate taxes and thus avoid the unnecessary liquidation of valuable growth and income-producing assets.
- ❑ **ESTATE PLANNING.** Ensure that your will and trust arrangements are up to date.
- ❑ **REVIEW.** Review your situation annually. Circumstances change.

Milestones

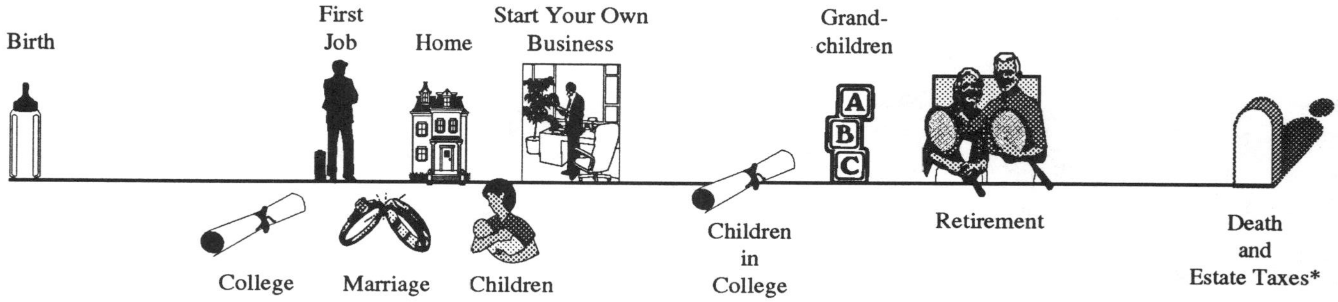

When is the best time to buy life insurance?

How much will you need?

How long will you need it?

How much will it cost?

* Unfortunately, death or disability could occur at any time.

The Need for Life Insurance is Permanent . . . Not Temporary.

YOU ARE DEAD!

What Does Your Family Do Now?

What Your Family Will Need To Know When You Die

- ❑ How much money is there?
- ❑ How much income is available and for how long?
- ❑ How much life insurance do you have? Where are the policies located?
- ❑ Where are your assets and important information located?
- ❑ Where do you want your money to go?
- ❑ Where are your will and any trust documents?
- ❑ Where do you wish to be buried?
- ❑ Is there a letter summarizing your wishes in addition to the will?
- ❑ Did you make any provisions for leaving money to a favorite charity or to a family foundation?
- ❑ What liabilities do you have and how are they to be paid?
- ❑ Which advisors (attorney, accountant, banker, insurance agent, investment advisor, stockbroker, etc.) should your family turn to for advice and to what extent?
- ❑ What will be the amount of the estate and inheritance taxes (if applicable) and how will they be paid? Is there life insurance specifically for this purpose?
- ❑ What are your plans for the continuation or disposition of your business?
- ❑ Where are the written plans and agreements regarding the business?
- ❑ Who will own the business?
- ❑ Who will manage the daily operations of the business?
- ❑ To what extent do you want your family involved in the business?
- ❑ What income is the business to provide to your family? How?
- ❑ Is there life insurance specifically for the use of the business?
- ❑ Are there any loans from family members to the business? How are they to be repaid?
- ❑ Are there any bank (or other) loans? How are they to be repaid?
- ❑ Are there any plans (written or otherwise) regarding the retention and compensation of key people?

Important Information for the ____________ Family

FAMILY MEMBERS	BIRTH DATE	PHONE	ADDRESS	COMMENTS

KEY PEOPLE	NAME	PHONE	COMMENTS
Guardians for Your Children			
Attorney			
Accountant			
Life Insurance Agent			
Stockbroker			
Financial Advisor			
Family Doctor			

LOCATION OF	
Business Agreements and Documents	
Wills and Trusts (Date Reviewed ______)	
Insurance Policies	
Safe Deposit Box, Key, and Number	

OTHER INFORMATION

Life Insurance Summary as of ____________

Insured	Company	Policy Number	Owner	Beneficiary	Amount	Type	Annual Premium	Cash Value	Waiver of Prem.	Comments

No One Has A Lease On Life!

On August 2nd, 1996, a Los Angeles television station carried a story about Marcia Clark and Christopher Darden, who were the prosecuting attorneys in the O.J. Simpson trial, attending a fund-raising event the prior evening for the Van Sloten family.

According to an article which appeared in the April 20th, 1996 issue of the *Los Angeles Times*, Martha Van Sloten, a 40-year-old legal secretary, had died in April from breast cancer which had spread into her bones. Her husband, Richard, who is 48, and who is a prosecuting attorney for Los Angeles County, has been diagnosed as having an inoperable brain tumor. Doctors say he'll be fortunate to live a few more months.

The Van Slotens have three daughters, one of whom is a 19-year-old who has been forced to drop out of college in order to help with her younger sisters who are ages 4 and 8. Arrangements have been made for the girls to live with relatives in Washington State. According to the article, the family's life insurance was modest.

What are the chances that even one spouse would die . . . let alone both? The chances are 100%. We just don't know when death will occur. No one has a lease on life. Life insurance must be purchased before you need it. By the time you know you need it . . . it's too late.

Have you recently reviewed your life insurance and your wills and trusts and guardianship arrangements? Wouldn't it make sense to do so right now?

Advisors

	ATTORNEY	CPA	INSURANCE AGENT
How paid	FEE	FEE	COMMISSION
Based on	TIME SPENT	TIME SPENT	RESULTS
Will act as the catalyst and coordinator with your CPA and attorney and save you thousands of dollars by assembling necessary background info, determining your goals and priorities, and developing the plan	NO	NO	YES
Will figure how much cash your family, business, and estate will ultimately need	MAYBE	MAYBE	YES
Will provide cash for your family	NO	NO	YES
Will provide cash for your business	NO	NO	YES
Will provide cash to pay estate taxes	NO	NO	YES
Will point out problems which insurance will solve	NO	NO	YES
Will be totally objective	NO*	NO*	NO*

* No one is totally objective because everyone has certain biases based on background. It is essential to differentiate between a professional and a personal opinion. *Integrity*, not *objectivity*, is the primary requisite for an advisor.

Time and Money

TIME is an acronym which stands for:

T axes
I nflation
M istakes
E mergencies

When trying to determine how much money you or your family will need in the event of death, disability, or retirement, these factors should be considered. When you take into account the impact of **Taxes**, the impact of **Inflation**, the fact that we sometimes make **Mistakes** with our investments, and that we may need to dip into capital for unforeseen **Emergencies**, we recommend that you use no more than a 3% real growth factor in determining how much money will be needed for a given period of time.

In a 40% income-tax bracket, 10% return is really 6%. If inflation is assumed to be 3%, the real growth is therefore 3%. This does not even take into account Mistakes and Emergencies. When it comes to planning for your family's financial future, it is better to be conservative than aggressive in your assumptions. It is far better to have too much money than not enough. Wouldn't you agree?

If you want to be conservative, we suggest assuming a real growth of zero per cent. Let's assume you were planning for your own retirement, and that you wanted $100,000 per year for the rest of your life starting at age 65. Let's also assume you plan on living 30 years. At age 65, you would need $100,000 per year multiplied by 30 years, or $3,000,000 of capital.

How Long Will $1,000,000 Last?

Year	Starting Capital	$50,000 After-Tax Income Adjusted for 3% Inflation	Remaining Capital	Remaining Capital Invested at 6% After Taxes
1	$1,000,000	$50,000	$950,000	$1,007,000
2	1,007,000	51,500	955,500	1,012,830
3	1,012,830	53,045	959,785	1,017,372
4	1,017,372	53,636	962,736	1,020,500
5	1,020,500	56,275	964,224	1,022,078
6	1,022,078	57,964	964,114	1,021,961
7	1,021,961	59,703	962,258	1,019,994
8	1,019,994	61,494	958,500	1,016,010
9	1,016,010	63,339	952,672	1,009,832
10	1,009,832	65,239	944,593	1,001,269
11	1,001,269	67,196	934,073	990,118
12	990,118	69,212	920,906	976,160
13	976,160	71,288	904,872	959,165
14	959,165	73,427	885,738	938,882
15	938,882	75,629	863,253	915,048
16	915,048	77,898	837,149	887,378
17	887,378	80,235	807,143	855,572
18	855,572	82,642	772,929	819,305
19	819,305	85,122	734,183	778,234
20	778,234	87,675	690,559	731,993
21	731,993	90,306	641,687	680,188
22	680,188	93,015	587,174	622,404
23	622,404	95,805	526,599	558,195
24	558,195	98,679	459,515	487,086
25	487,086	101,640	385,447	408,573
26	408,573	104,689	303,885	322,118
27	322,118	107,830	214,288	227,145
28	227,145	111,064	116,081	123,046
29	123,046	114,396	8,649	9,168
30	9,168	117,828	BROKE!	BROKE!

Life Insurance . . . The 1% Solution

Why Not Position 1% Per Year to Provide Protection for Your Family and Your Business?

- ❏ **ESTATE TAX FUNDING.** Why not let 1% of your estate each year help protect the other 99%?
- ❏ **KEY MANAGEMENT PROTECTION.** Why not let 1% of your sales each year help protect the other 99%?
- ❏ **BUY AND SELL FUNDING.** Why not let 1% of your business' value each year help protect the other 99%?
- ❏ **LOAN REPAYMENT.** Payment of an additional 1% each year on top of the interest you are paying would ensure the ability to repay the loan in the event of death.
- ❏ **FAMILY INCOME.** If you need $1,000,000 to provide income for your family when you die, why not set aside 1% per year to help provide the protection?
- ❏ **DISABILITY INCOME.** If you are now making $200,000 annually, why not set aside 2% annually to purchase disability income protection?
- ❏ **WEALTH ACCUMULATION.** If you want to accumulate $1,000,000 for your future, why not invest 1% or 2% annually? $10,000 per year for 30 years at 7% = $1,000,000. $20,000 per year for 20 years at 8% = $1,000,000.

NOTE: Depending upon the specifics of the situation, 1% may not do the job. It may take 2% or more . . . but the number is almost always peanuts compared to the problem which it solves.

Forbes Beats Tax Man with Insurance Buys

BOSTON (AP) - Insurance policies designed to protect Malcolm Forbes' estate from the taxman may have proved to be the bon vivant businessman's last capitalist tool.

Insurance companies that originally balked at paying millions of dollars in claims to the estate have paid up, a Forbes official said Friday.

The late publisher of the business magazine dubbed "capitalist tool" reportedly took out millions of dollars in life insurance with different companies in the years preceding his death in February at age 70.

> ***Garson said Forbes often commented that the only way to pass on an estate worth any money when he died was to have large amounts of life insurance.***

Forbes died of an apparent heart attack at Timberfield, his Far Hills, N.J., mansion. But John Hancock Mutual Insurance Company last month withheld payment on a multi-million-dollar policy pending an investigation into the claim.

Hancock officials had said only that an investigation was being conducted, but published reports indicated medical information provided by Forbes was being examined.

But Hancock spokesman Richard Bevilacqua said the company had completed its "routine" investigation and paid the claim. Forbes spokesman Don Garson said all pending insurance claims have been paid to the Forbes estate.

Neither spokesman would discuss the amounts of money involved, but Garson said that the previously reported figure of $46 million in total insurance claims was too low.

"Forbes is an exceptionally valuable property. That ($46 million) seems like a drop in the bucket," he said. Garson said Forbes often commented that the only way to pass on an estate worth any money when he died was to have large amounts of life insurance.

Estimates of Forbes' estate range from $400 million to $1 billion. The estate would be taxed in the 55 percent brackets according to tax specialists. But much of Forbes' estate, such as the magazine and his art collection, could not go on the auction block to pay the government.

Forbes' apparent solution was to take out insurance policies, some within the last two years, to pay the necessary cash.

Garson said no discrepancies were discovered in the medical information Forbes provided to Hancock. "I can assure you all investigations have been completed. There were no irregularities . . . and the claims have all been paid," he said.

Bevilacqua would not discuss the details of the agreement between Hancock and the Forbes estate, which he said was concluded Tuesday.

Source: *Dayton Daily News,* Sat., June 9, 1990

Why Affluent Individuals Acquire Life Insurance

Why do affluent individuals who are worth $5,000,000 or $10,000,000 or $20,000,000 or even $100,000,000 or more acquire life insurance? Does life insurance really make sense for them and their families?

Most wealthy people would prefer that their estates go to their children rather than to 260,000,000 strangers. They also know the IRS is not going to build a building with their name on it. Giving money to the IRS in the form of estate taxes is not a very effective means of benefitting society.

The wealthy have a lot more to lose than do others. Your estate is the tangible representation of your lifetime. You spend a lifetime building your estate, and then when you die, the IRS estate tax collector can take away 50% or more of your lifetime of effort virtually overnight. The estate taxes are due and payable in cash within nine months of your death. Could you write a check today for up to 50% or more of everything you own without it hurting just a little bit? If you can't write that check . . . how will your children be able to write it? On the other hand, if you could write a check for about 1% or 2% of what you own each year, the insurance company will ultimately write a check which can be used to help pay the estate taxes.

Some people are concerned that inheriting a lot of money will ruin their children. Malcolm Forbes started with an inheritance and built on that. He then purchased huge insurance policies to help minimize the tax impact on his estate, so that he could pass the inheritance on to his children. There is never too much money . . . only too little character. Do you think that paying estate taxes will build character?

Everyone pays the price for success . . . not just the breadwinner. You pay the price, your spouse pays the price, your children pay the price, and your employees pay the price. Everyone pays. Why compound the problem by having them pay the price again in the form of estate taxes when you are gone? Why should your dreams die when you die, if there is an option?

Life insurance represents a viable alternative to the liquidation of

Why Affluent Individuals Acquire Life Insurance

(continued)

your lifetime. It normally can be acquired without changing your lifestyle. Most individuals think of buying life insurance out of cash flow, and thus the cost seems to be prohibitive when large amounts of insurance are being considered. In larger estates, insurance is acquired by repositioning capital or using part of the growth. This generally results in a greater return after income taxes and after estate taxes than would be achieved in any other form of investment.

Doesn't it make more sense to set aside a little bit today during your lifetime rather than transferring a massive problem to your children tomorrow? If you can't handle a small problem today, how can they handle a much larger problem tomorrow? No one likes to buy life insurance. It is simply the lesser of two evils.

Even if you had adequate cash available to pay the estate taxes, it would not seem to make sense to use it if you could discount the estate tax liability by 80% or more using life insurance. Why pay $1,000,000 if you only need to pay $200,000? Wouldn't you rather pay wholesale than retail? Why be forced to sell a cash cow if you could sell just a little milk instead?

The current tax law enables a decedent to leave his or her entire estate to the surviving spouse without incurring any estate tax. As a result of the "sucker play," as it has been labeled by several top estate planning attorneys, many wealthy individuals have been lulled into a false sense of security. The tax is merely deferred until the death of the surviving spouse. The tax must still be paid. The problem still exists. In many situations, it makes sense to pay taxes at the first death.

Why do affluent individuals acquire life insurance? It is just plain common sense to spread payments over time when that will enable you to avoid a large loss all at once. Why not let 1% of your estate each year protect the other 99%?

The best way to determine whether or not life insurance makes sense for you is to look at the numbers and examine your options.

An Attorney's Point of View

The Value of Life Insurance in Estate Planning

BY ROBERT E. HALES, ESQ.

I have personally been involved in the preparation of over 5,000 living trusts, and having done that many estate plans in the last seventeen years and having taught the subject for six years at Santa Clara Law School, I can only reach one conclusion as to the role the life insurance product plays in the estate planning process. It is impossible to properly plan without it.

Many of my colleagues devote a great deal of time to showing their clients how to minimize the consequences of tax at the death of a husband or wife. Some of them, unfortunately, too few, even attempt to show their clients how to avoid unnecessary legal procedures, such as probates and conservatorships. Some even try to do in-depth designing of the estate plan to try and preserve the family land, farm or business, for, not just their children, but their grandchildren. It is my opinion that regardless of how much time and documentation is spent on the above estate planning problems, the estate planning attorney has not completed his services to the client until one very important question has been asked, and answered, prior to the clients' deaths.

What is curious is, my clients have their automobiles insured so that they do not have to use their money to replace them in a time of loss, but they usually don't have themselves insured which is a certain loss as compared to the automobile which is an improbable loss.

The answer to the question, "Whose money do I use?" is, we will either use the client's money, or the insurance company's money. Please keep in mind as the attorney, it really isn't that important whose money is used to pay taxes because the money doesn't belong to the attorney. But it makes no sense to me to use the client's money if insurance monies are available.

For example, if I have kept a $2 million estate free of probate, and I have minimized the death taxes and I have designed a plan that will assure the assets will pass to whom the clients directed, what good is all of this, if at the time of the death of my clients, it is necessary for their beneficiaries to liquidate almost half of everything that the clients owned?

What is curious is, my clients have their automobiles insured so that they do not have to use their money to replace them in a time of loss, but they usually don't have themselves insured which is a certain loss as compared to the automobile which is an improbable loss.

I had a client once who owned 60 single-dwelling homes. I asked him,

The Value of Life Insurance in Estate Planning

(continued)

"whose money do we use to pay death taxes?" He answered that all he had were his homes. Not having given it much thought before, he was curious as to how many of his homes would have to be sold to pay his death taxes.

I noted approximately 30 to 35, recognizing that selling 30 homes in nine months would probably deflate that market, not counting the costs of selling those homes. I asked him to list the homes that would need to be sold. When he got to number 10, he found it very difficult to continue.

I told him to stop and go back to the top of his list and just sell the first three homes he checked. "Can I pay all of my death taxes just by selling three homes?" he queried. "You told me you would have to sell 35."

I said, "Yes, that's the difference."

"If you will sell the three homes now to get enough equity out of your estate to purchase all the life insurance you need to pay your death taxes, your family won't have to sell 35 homes when you die."

An interesting fact about that situation is that his two adult sons were present and when the father began to think about whether he should sell three homes now or 35 later on, his oldest son looked at him and said: "Dad, you aren't really going to think about that, are you?"

So many times, estate planning attorneys have reduced taxes, eliminated probate, and have seen to it that the estate is distributed as the clients wanted. But in so many cases, we have seen that those beneficiaries have had to sell the 35 homes instead of the father selling the three. Isn't it easier for someone to sell $20,000 of stock to buy a million dollar policy than it is for the attorney to sell a million dollars worth of stock to pay the death taxes? Isn't it easier for the dairy person to sell five cows a year to pay his insurance premiums than it is for an attorney to sell his whole herd when he dies?

If clients can be made to see these choices, and if clients can be made to see the ultimate liquidation of their estates vs. the partial liquidation to pay insurance premiums, in my opinion, the attorney, not the life underwriter, is then fully doing his job in the estate planning process.

Mr. Hales is an attorney whose practice is devoted entirely to estate and business planning. His firm, Hales, Hales & George, has offices in San Francisco and Saratoga, California.

The Zero Estate Tax Plan

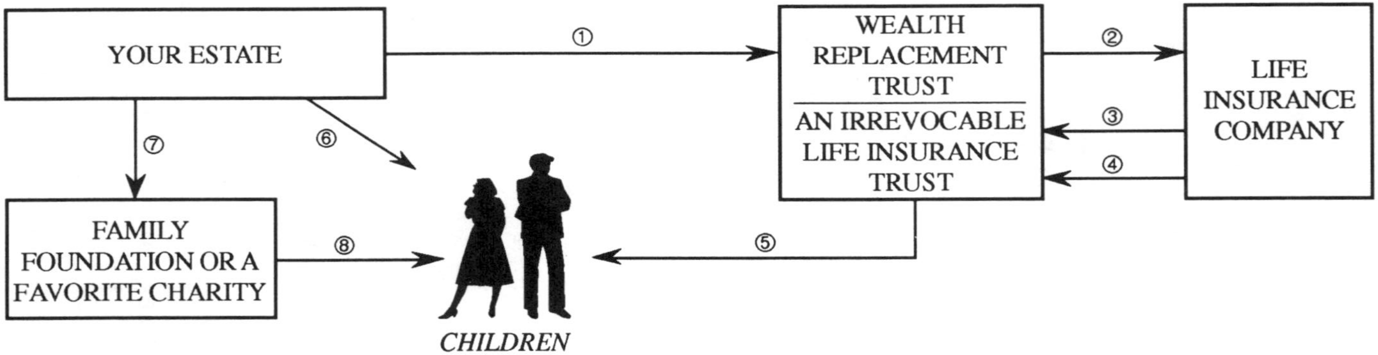

① During the parents' lives, gifts are made to an irrevocable life insurance trust.

② The gifts are used to pay premiums for insurance on either or both parents.

③ The cash value is reflected as an asset of the trust.

④ At death, the insurance is paid to the trust.

⑤ According to the terms of the trust, the money from the insurance is paid to the children.

⑥ The children receive $1,200,000 ($600,000 per parent) which can pass with proper planning without estate taxes.

⑦ The balance of the estate is left without being subject to estate taxes to a family foundation which then provides money for various charitable purposes or to a favorite charity.

⑧ The children run the foundation and are paid reasonable compensation. If the money were left to a charity, the children would receive no compensation.

When the Man is the Company

Sikes Corp. had its bankers nervous ten years ago. Jimmy Sikes, chief executive officer, had plunged the Lakeland, FL ceramic-tile maker into carpet manufacture. That was a disaster. Sikes dropped $11 million during a period when sales ran at only $45 million. Sikes' bankers agreed to stand by, and they weren't unhappy that the company bought key-man insurance on Jimmy Sikes' life. He was, after all, the company.

The multimillion-dollar policy cost a yearly premium of $200,000 – tough on the company, especially in years such as 1976, when earnings were only $370,000. As earnings improved, however, paying the premium became less of a hardship. "It was just another of the costs of doing business," says Phil Dunne, chief financial officer of Sikes.

Then, on a Saturday afternoon last August, sitting by his pool, Jimmy Sikes had chest pains. His wife and 18-year-old son drove him to an emergency room and he walked in, expecting to undergo a few tests. Twenty-five minutes later, at the age of 52, he was dead of a heart attack.

The insurance policy, still in force, paid $6.9 million to Sikes Corp. in September. The tax-free payment will add $3.12 per share to the company's estimated 45 cents a share earnings on operations for fiscal 1983, ended Feb. 28.

It also gives the company time to breathe. "Without it, our bankers would have had to be very concerned," says Dunne. At the time, the balance sheet was loaded with $21 million of high-interest debt, most acquired in 1981 to build an ultra-efficient new plant (see Forbes, July 5, 1982). Though revenues are holding steady – they were an estimated $50 million in fiscal 1983 – profits have fallen for the last two years because of the slump in housing construction. There was little doubt about using the insurance money right away to reduce the company's swollen debt to a manageable 35% of total capital.

Of course, key-man insurance wouldn't do for every company what it did for Sikes. "It's most useful," says Dunne, "in cases like ours – companies that are highly leveraged or dominated by one person." With 1982 profits of $169 million, Gulf & Western would have hardly noticed the money had it held a $6.9 million policy on Charles Bluhdorn. And the bureaucracy at most large companies is designed to keep the loss of an individual from threatening the whole.

Even at Sikes, other circumstances eased the transition. Since the Sikes family owns 30% of the common shares and most of the voting shares, there was no takeover threat. Jimmy Sikes had moved several years ago to install professional managers, after foreseeing a management gap. His 82-year-old father had been out of the business for years; his brother, Leon Jr., preferred to run a distributorship of the company and his own children would be too young for years. As a result, Kelly Norton, who became CEO after Sikes' death, had actually run day-to-day operations for nearly four years. "There was never any question of selling out," Norton says.

In the near future, management will have its hands full trying to restore sales growth and profits. But it's no wonder that once again the company is preparing for the unthinkable. Dunne expects to sign papers this month for two key-man policies, probably with a total face value of $4 million. One is for Kelly Norton, the other for Jimmy Sikes' brother, Leon, who is now chairman of the board. "We don't have somebody who could step right into either one of those jobs, and if – God forbid – something should happen," says Dunne, "then we'd need all the help we could get." - Laura Saunders

Source: Forbes (March 28, 1983). Reprinted with permission of Forbes.

How Much Will A College Education Cost?

AGE OF CHILD NOW	YEARS TO COLLEGE	ANNUAL COST *	FOUR YEAR COST **	ANNUAL INVESTMENT REQUIRED @ 8%
18	0	$10,000	$40,000	$40,000
17	1	10,800	43,200	40,000
16	2	11,664	46,656	20,769
15	3	12,597	50,388	14,371
14	4	13,605	54,420	11,182
13	5	14,693	58,772	9,276
12	6	15,869	63,476	8,012
11	7	17,138	68,552	7,145
10	8	18,509	74,036	6,445
9	9	19,990	79,960	5,929
8	10	21,589	86,356	5,520
7	11	23,316	93,264	5,188
6	12	25,182	100,728	4,915
5	13	27,196	108,784	4,686
4	14	29,372	117,488	4,492
3	15	31,722	126,888	4,327
2	16	34,259	137,036	4,184
1	17	37,000	148,000	4,060
0	18	39,960	159,840	3,952

* Adjusted for 8% cost increase annually.

** This is the cost discounted at 8%.

EXAMPLE: If your child is now 8 years old, what now costs $10,000 will cost over $21,000. To accumulate the four-year cost, which will exceed $86,000, you will need to invest $5,520 annually at 8%. If the cost today were $20,000, as opposed to $10,000, you would need to invest twice as much starting now (2 x $5,520 = $11,040 per year).

The Power of Compound Interest

$100,000 One-Time Investment

Years	Annual Compound Rate of Return				
	4%	**6%**	**8%**	**10%**	**12%**
10	$148,024	$179,085	$215,893	$259,374	$310,585
20	219,112	320,714	466,096	672,750	964,629
30	324,340	574,349	1,006,266	1,744,940	2,995,992
40	480,102	1,028,572	2,172,452	4,525,926	9,305,097

$10,000 Annual Investment

Years	Annual Compound Rate of Return				
	4%	**6%**	**8%**	**10%**	**12%**
10	$124,864	$139,716	$156,455	$175,312	$196,546
20	309,692	389,927	494,229	630,025	806,987
30	583,283	838,017	1,223,459	1,809,434	2,702,926
40	988,265	1,640,477	2,797,810	4,868,518	8,591,424

How Long Will it Take to Accumulate $1,000,000?

Annual Investment	Annual Compound Rate of Return				
	4%	**6%**	**8%**	**10%**	**12%**
$5,000	56 Years	44 Years	36 Years	31 Years	28 Years
10,000	41 Years	33 Years	28 Years	25 Years	22 Years
15,000	33 Years	27 Years	24 Years	21 Years	19 Years
20,000	28 Years	24 Years	21 Years	18 Years	17 Years

Annual Investment Required to Accumulate $1,000,000

Years	Annual Compound Rate of Return				
	4%	**6%**	**8%**	**10%**	**12%**
10	$80,087	$71,574	$63,916	$57,041	$50,879
20	32,290	25,646	20,234	15,872	12,392
30	17,144	11,933	8,174	5,527	3,700
40	10,119	6,096	3,574	2,054	1,164

These numbers are purely hypothetical. They are for illustrative purposes only and are not intended to represent any specific investment or to imply that any specific investment will achieve the results shown.

Comparing Various Financial Vehicles

Financial Vehicle	Principal	Term	Interest Rate	Annual Payment
❑ Mortgage	$1,000,000	30 Years	8%	$88,000
❑ Certificates of Deposit	$1,000,000	5 Years	6%	$60,000
❑ Treasury Bonds	$1,000,000	30 Years	7%	$70,000
❑ Life Insurance* $1,000,000 (Age 55)	$1,000,000	1 Year	2,757%	$35,000
The rate of return is determined by the year in which death occurs.	1,360,000	10 Years	23.83%	35,000
	2,200,000	20 Years	9.98%	35,000
	3,690,000	30 Years	7.22%	35,000
	6,530,000	40 Years	6.49%	35,000

* These figures are based on current assumptions and are not guaranteed.

"It's unwise to pay too much, but it's worse to pay too little. When you pay too much, you lose a little money . . . that is all. When you pay too little, you sometimes lose everything, because the thing you bought was incapable of doing the thing it was bought to do. The common law of business balance prohibits paying a little and getting a lot. It can't be done. If you deal with the lowest bidder, it is well to add something for the risk you run, and if you do that . . . you will have enough to pay for something better."

JOHN RUSKIN

About the Author

Born in Baltimore, Maryland, Howard Wight graduated from the U.S. Naval Academy in 1961. Following service in the Navy Supply Corps, which included a tour of duty with the Seabees in Vietnam, he joined Connecticut General in 1969 in San Francisco.

While associated with a Palo Alto financial planning firm, Howard did seminars on stock options and financial planning for such prestigious companies as Hewlett-Packard and Intel. He was an agent with Northwestern Mutual from 1973-1990. In 1983, he started publishing the Wight Financial Concepts Newsletter, to which many of the top insurance and financial advisors in the country subscribe. Howard has become the life insurance advisors' advisor.

Howard Wight conducts about 50 seminars annually in the United States, Canada, and Europe on selling, motivation, success, and time management. He was a featured speaker at the 1987, 1988, 1991, and 1994 Million Dollar Round Table annual meetings. He is also the author of *Success and Time Management, Red-Letter Language,* and *Life's Lessons.*

Howard Wight, CLU, ChFC
Wight Financial Concepts Corporation
1330 Jones Street, Suite 404
San Francisco, CA 94109
800-486-SELL